Unwrap the Memories:
Nostalgic Christmas Stories to Warm the Heart

By

Andrew L. Luna, Ph.D.

Unwrap the Memories: Nostalgic Christmas Stories to Warm the Heart

Copyright © 2016 by Andrew L. Luna

andrew-luna@comcast.com
Facebook/Andrew L. Luna

Published in the United States

First Edition
10 9 8 7 6 5 4 3 2 1

ISBN
Paperback: 978-0-9981261-0-4
EPUB: 978-0-9981261-1-1

Cover design and inside illustrations created by Chelsea O'Mara Holeman

Dedication

This book is dedicated to my loving wife, Danita, and our wonderful twins Jay and Jessica. May the spirit and warmth of Christmas always be with you.

Preface

Unfortunately, Christmas has become more hectic and stressful than ever before, and people who celebrate the season have little time to devote to relaxation and celebration of the true meaning of this special holiday. When they do find a little time, they are often bombarded by the commercialism and bawdiness of Xmas rather than the warmth and benevolence of Christmas.

I, too, have experienced this same problem. On those few occasions when I relax by the tree, I am inundated by Christmas programs on television that do little to relax me. I mean, who really wants to watch "Santa Claus Conquers the Martians" or "Bad Santa?" And just how warm and cozy is the slasher movie "Silent Night, Bloody Night" anyway? Magazines during the season are not much better, either. They are more interested in what I should cook or how I should plan my next party, which further increases my level of stress and anxiety. To me, part of Christmas should be spent with the simpler pleasures in life like the sharing and reading of timeless, wholesome Christmas stories.

As a former newspaper editor, I had written a few Christmas stories over the years. Friends and family told me I should write more. Therefore, I decided to write a collection of my Christmas memories to share with those who feel the same way about the season as I do. While these short stories are about me, my family, and things I like about Christmas, they are not unique to me. Just about any family should be able to relate, in some small way, to the experience of tasting boiled custard after Christmas dinner, watching Christmas shoppers in the mall as they frantically buy their last-minute presents, or taking a moment to be a child again in reverence to our Savior who was born that night in a manger.

This book is a self-published effort. I had a difficult time getting an actual publisher to market it. I guess the stories are not sensational, gruesome, or salacious enough for their perceived target readership. So, to those of you who bought this book, I sincerely appreciate it, and I hope you find the joy and inspiration in reading it, as I had, in writing it.

While writing can be a lonely endeavor, a good book can only come with the help of others. To that end, I would like to personally thank Chelsea O'Mara Holeman who designed the cover and inside illustrations; Christa Raney, friend and colleague at the University of North Alabama, who provided her professional editing talents; and my wife, Danita, and daughter, Jessica who also served as proofreaders. Without their work and talents, this book would not have been completed.

I designed this book to where the reader can enjoy one story per day through the month of December. I like to think of it as a daily appetizer or midnight snack as you catch a little quiet time for yourself. Now, you may want to read most of the book in one sitting. That's ok. Just don't read it hurriedly. As you finish each story, reflect on what Christmas really means to you and how you can share that feeling with your friends and family.

Now, I would be remiss if I didn't pay tribute to the two most important Christmas stories ever told. They are the stories in the Bible of Christ's birth as told by Luke and Matthew. While there are many versions of the Bible out there, I am especially fond of the King James Version. There is a musical quality to it that is unique to any other version. Moreover, it is the version I remember my mom reading to me as a kid as I gazed up at our brightly lighted Christmas tree or looked down at Mary, Joseph, and the Babe lying in our manger by the fireplace in our den. In short, these two special stories help me unwrap my special Christmas memories. Merry Christmas, everyone!

Luke 2: 1-20

And it came to pass in those days, that there went out a decree from Caesar Augustus, that all the world should be taxed. (And this taxing was first made when Cyrenius was governor of Syria.) And all went to be taxed, every one into his own city. And Joseph also went up from Galilee, out of the city of Nazareth, into Judaea, unto the city of David, which is called Bethlehem; (because he was of the house and lineage of David:) To be taxed with Mary his espoused wife, being great with child. And so it was, that, while they were there, the days were accomplished that she should be delivered. And she brought forth her firstborn son, and wrapped him in swaddling clothes, and laid him in a manger; because there was no room for them in the inn. And there were in the same country shepherds abiding in the field, keeping watch over their flock by night. And, lo, the angel of the Lord came upon them, and the glory of the Lord shone round about them: and they were sore afraid. And the angel said unto them, Fear not: for, behold, I bring you good tidings of great joy, which shall be to all people. For unto you is born this day in the city of David a Savior, which is Christ the Lord. And this shall be a sign unto you; ye shall find the babe wrapped in swaddling clothes, lying in a manger. And suddenly there was with the angel a multitude of the heavenly host praising God, and saying, Glory to God in the highest, and on earth peace, good will toward men. And it came to pass, as the angels were gone away from them into heaven, the shepherds said one to another, Let us now go even unto Bethlehem, and see this thing which is come to pass, which the Lord hath made known unto us. And they came with haste, and found Mary, and Joseph, and the babe lying in a manger. And when they had seen it, they made known abroad the saying which was told them concerning this child. And all they that heard it wondered at those things which were told them by the shepherds. But Mary kept all these things, and pondered them in her heart. And the shepherds returned, glorifying and praising God for all the things that they had heard and seen, as it was told unto them.

Matthew 2: 1-12

Now when Jesus was born in Bethlehem of Judaea in the days of Herod the king, behold, there came wise men from the east to Jerusalem, saying, "Where is he that is born King of the Jews? For we have seen his star in the east, and are come to worship him." When Herod the king had heard these things, he was troubled, and all Jerusalem with him. And when he had gathered all the chief priests and scribes of the people together, he demanded of them where Christ should be born. And they said unto him, In Bethlehem of Judaea: for thus it is written by the prophet, and thou Bethlehem, in the land of Juda, art not the least among the princes of Juda: for out of thee shall come a Governor, that shall rule my people Israel. Then Herod, when he had privily called the wise men, inquired of them diligently what time the star appeared. And he sent them to Bethlehem, and said, Go and search diligently for the young child; and when ye have found him, bring me word again, that I may come and worship him also. When they had heard the king, they departed; and, lo, the star, which they saw in the east, went before them, till it came and stood over where the young child was. When they saw the star, they rejoiced with exceeding great joy. And when they were come into the house, they saw the young child with Mary his mother, and fell down, and worshiped him: and when they had opened their treasures, they presented unto him gifts; gold, and frankincense and myrrh. And being warned of God in a dream that they should not return to Herod, they departed into their own country another way.

###

December 1

Unwrapping Memories

It is the Christmas season again, and if you are like me, just about everything you see, smell, taste, or hear rekindles pleasant memories of the past – whether it be long ago or just last year. With this awakening, the holiday celebration takes on a complexity of emotions and sentiments much like the layering of flavors in a favorite homemade soup. As each year passes, feelings about the season develop and mature, and Christmas takes on a more intrinsic and clearer meaning. What once was personal and simple when we were younger, Christmas has now become more meaningful and selfless as we grow older. In unwrapping the memories of our past, though, we continue to relive part of our child-like excitement and wonder in homage to the small Child in a manger.

There are so many memory gifts that I enjoy unwrapping during the holidays. To me, part of the joy and delight of the season is recapturing what was special and new to me when I was younger. Every time I open the old, yellowed box of Shiny Brite ornaments that was handed down to me by my parents, I step back to a time when I could barely reach the middle of the tree, much less the top. Every bite I take of the seven layer cookies that my mom used to bake, and which my wife has now perfected, I remember the warm hug and cold glass of milk that mom would give me as I looked at our tree in quiet serenity. Each time I sit by a warm fire during the season, I am doubly warmed by the emotions of that special Christmas Eve when I asked my wife to marry me.

Some of my memory gifts are large while others are quite small. Some evoke feelings of happiness and joy while others I unwrap are more moving and poignant. Now that I live in Florence, Alabama, I have the opportunity to drive by the house where my grandmother was born and raised and where my dad was also raised. This is the house where many of my younger Christmas memories began. Just seeing it reminds me of warmth, laughter, holiday dinners, and hard Christmas candy in assorted colors and flavors. These emotions are soon dampened by reality because none of my family now lives in that house that we once called home so many years ago.

Passing by the old house, I look up at the second story to the corner bedroom window facing East Mobile and Walnut streets. Catty-cornered from her house was the old Sears and Roebuck building. It is a vacant lot now. Often, we would celebrate Thanksgiving at grandmother's. After dinner and when it was time for bed, I would sleep in that room. Early Friday morning, I would awake to the sound of a helicopter buzzing over the house. I would jump out of bed and race over to the window because I knew it meant only one thing; Santa Claus was being flown in to start the Christmas shopping season! Each time I hear the crooning intimacy of Bing Crosby's *White Christmas*; the relaxed, incandescent voice of Nat King Cole's *The Christmas Song*; or the unique recitations of Walter Brennen in *A Farmer's Christmas Prayer*; I remember helping mom with her gift wrapping by picking out the paper and bows while the aroma of freshly baked fruitcake cookies wafted through our home. There are Christmas hymns that take me back to my beautifully decorated church as we celebrated on the eve of Christ's birth, or to my high school choir as we started to practice in September for our annual Christmas concert. The laughter of small children running over to meet Santa reminds me of the toys he brought for me during my younger years. I can still hear my Varoom bicycle as I first raced up and down the streets in my neighborhood on that cold, clear Christmas morn. I remember the long expanse of plastic, orange track I laid out in the living room while racing my Hot Wheels cars and making sure the cat didn't attack the winner before he crossed the finish line. I remember how high my Super Ball bounced, how cool the blinking purple light was on top of my Major Matt Mason Space Station, and how many neat experiments were in my chemistry set. In short, it was so much fun being a kid at Christmas, that I didn't think anything could be better. However, as the years passed, I was able to witness the joy and excitement in our twins as they ran into the den to see what Santa had brought them. The pleasure I experienced seeing them tear into their toys and games and of hearing their laughter and excitement as they ran through the house was infinitely better to me than any Christmas gift I ever received.

Much like the gifts piled around our tree, my memories of Christmas continue to please and comfort me in both their quantity and variety. Some will always be large and at the forefront of my mind. Others, I accidentally may stumble upon while rekindling long-forgotten remembrances. Moreover, with each new Christmas, more special times happen with the people I love and treasure. These are the memories to be wrapped up now and opened later while experiencing the joy of future Christmases.

I love Christmas and all of the warmth and joy I experience while celebrating the birth of our Savior with my family and friends. As I grow older, I remember fondly the Christmases of yesterday and look forward to creating new memories in the future.

###

December 2

Putting Up the Decorations

Usually, during the Thanksgiving Holiday, I haul down the tree, lights, and other trimmings from the attic in preparation for the ritual of decorating our house for Christmas. As I bring down each box, I realize that the gap between putting the decorations away and getting them back down again seems to get shorter with each passing year. I look around at the labels on the boxes that describe their contents. I remember when my wife first put most of those labels on back in the early 90's. Seems like it was just yesterday.

Many years ago, we bought a huge 10-foot tall artificial tree. My wife bought two large plastic storage boxes just to store it. I still kid her about those boxes. I call them body storage containers because an average sized person could easily fit inside them. Those two boxes are the first that come down. When

I attach the pole to base of the tree, I then pull each branch from the box. I bend and shape it as best I can to make it look natural before I attach it to the tree. I keep doing this until I get to the top. Rather than smaller branches, the top quarter of the tree is all one piece. I put this topper on the tree and then adjust the limbs so the tree won't look like it just got out of bed and forgot to comb its hair.

Putting this tree together, I'm reminded of the first tree my wife and I had. It was a five footer that could be put up in just a few minutes. However, it was a handsome little tree, and we had just as much enjoyment from that little pine as if it were the tallest tree in the neighborhood. Now that the assembly of our larger tree has been completed, I unwrap our porcelain angel, climb up three or four rungs of the ladder, and place her at the very top of our tree. All Christmas trees should have an angel or star atop them to proclaim the birth of our Lord.

We had used a star for many years. One day, however, when we were shopping for decorations, I saw the angel and wanted to try it. Well, as fate would have it, as we were walking to our vehicle with our newly bought decorations, my wife accidentally dropped the angel in the parking lot. I heard a breaking sound, and opening the bag, I saw a headless angel. We took her home, and with love and care, I pieced together the angel's head with glue. I did an ok job with the exception of some small pieces toward the back of her head that I couldn't find. From that point forward, our new angle was given the name Head Wound Harriet.

The next items to go on the tree are the lights. For years, we had the miniature lights, and they looked pretty on the smaller tree. To me, they just didn't give enough punch to our larger tree, so I bought the traditional C6 lights that have been used on Christmas trees for many years. As I string the lights, I'm careful not to have too many of the same color close together. I also have to be careful that our cat doesn't get the chance to pounce on the unattached part of the string dragging the floor behind me. Even though I'm well into my adult years, I still feel the excitement of a kid when I turn on the lights for the very first time during the season. The warm glow takes me back to simpler times and quickly turns our den into a holiday showplace.

I have recently seen all of the LED and digital lighting inventions of today's decorations. I personally don't like them. Their color tint is too much on the blue side for me, and their automations and color changes remind me too much of fairground lights or signage along the Las Vegas Strip. To me, Christmas lights should be warmer and more natural looking. However, everyone has his or her own taste in decorations. I'm just glad that I can still get the old stuff.

With that said, I'm old enough to remember when Christmas lights were wired in a series rather than a parallel configuration. The old way of wiring meant that if one bulb burned out, none of the others would work. I remember we would carefully check each string before we put it on the tree to make sure it worked. If it didn't, we would have to tighten each bulb into the socket. If that didn't work, we had to painstakingly replace each bulb with one we knew that worked until the string lighted. I don't miss those times.

I then pull down another body storage container from the attic. This one contains all the ornaments for our tree. Now, some people like to have themes for their tree. Some like to coordinate their tree with only one or two colors. Some like the natural look of holly, red berries, and pine cones. Still others like a tree with variety. We fit into that category. In fact, to say that our tree is eclectic is quite an understatement. There is something for every taste on our tree. We have everything from natural-looking poinsettia leaves to the Disney character, Goofy, playing Jacob Marley from Dickens' *A Christmas Carol*. In short, our tree is a fun and happy one.

For years, my wife and I would make sure we would buy a dated ornament that would signify something special in our lives that year. The first ornament we got was one with two hearts on it that proudly proclaims "Our First Christmas Together." We bought that one when we first got engaged. Then there is the ornament with the little red bird in a house that marks our first house. We had worked so hard to earn the down payment for that house. I remember our first Christmas in it. It was a very happy time for us. There are also ornaments signifying the various places we lived, vacations we took, and important wedding anniversaries. We have a new millennium ornament as well as ornaments representing the various colleges where I worked. To us the most important ornaments are a little pink bear and little blue bear I bought for my wife 18 years ago that are inscribed "Baby's First Christmas" in honor of our new twins.

Placing each one of these ornaments on the tree usually sparks recollections of past Christmases and prompts conversations and laughter while we listen to Christmas music or watch a favorite Christmas movie. Everyone participates in putting the ornaments on the tree, and everyone has his or her favorite. We have actually had to stop buying ornaments because we have run out of room on our giant tree. As our son and daughter move off to start their own lives, I sure hope that they may want a few of our ornaments to rekindle some of their Christmas memories.

The tree is now up, and the boxes put away. We decorate the other parts of our house and ready ourselves for the season. Our daughter has included a whimsical little pink tree in her room with some strange decorations on it, including peppermint lights and ornaments that look like a pizza slice and a bottle of mustard. Each time she buys a new ornament, she is filled with the same excitement as I used to have when I was younger, and for a moment, I slip into a childlike happiness.

To me, putting up Christmas decorations rekindles the past while stimulating anticipation for the future. It is a time when families start to celebrate the joy of the season through their little traditions and customs. It is a time when innocence and laughter should prevail. In short, decorating for Christmas should bring out the kid in each one of us. After all, we are celebrating the birth of the Christ Child.

###

December 3

Gemütlichkeit

Many of our Christmas traditions came from Germany. Take the Christmas tree, for example. The father of the Protestant movement, Martin Luther, was a monk for much of his life during the 16th century until his transformation. As the story goes, he was walking in the woods one cold, clear night around Christmastime. He was admiring all of the tress with the stars twinkling in the background. He then noticed that, if he stood to where a tree was between him and the sky, the stars seemed to be part of the tree. This gave him an idea. He brought a tree indoors and decorated it with candles to mimic the brilliant starlight from outside.

By the mere fact that Luther lighted his tree with candles, we can say that the Germans started the tradition of Christmas lights as well. Tinsel is also a creation of Deutschland. Around 1910, metallic strings were made to wrap around the Christmas tree to emulate icicles on a cold winter's night. The first tinsel was made with real silver and very fragile to the touch. To make the strands stronger, lead was used, which, later, turned out not to be a very good idea.

The multicolored ornaments that are a staple to a properly decorated Christmas tree originated from Germany. In 1597, Hans Greiner was living in Lauscha, which is a picturesque town located in a valley of the Thüringer Schiefergebirge mountain range. Lauscha is widely known for its glassworks, and Greiner came up with the idea of blowing decorative glass balls (called baubles) to be placed on the tree. His idea became such a big hit that other glassmakers in the area followed suite, and the Christmas ornament gained prominence worldwide.

Germany is also attributed for the green and red colors of Christmas. Long ago in many German towns during Christmas Eve (Heiligabend), festive plays were performed in homage to the season. To decorate the stage, boughs of evergreen were used to symbolize the Garden of Eden. Red apples tied to the boughs represented the forbidden fruit.

Nutcracker figurines originated in the Erzebirge area of Germany as early as the 1700's. They were traditionally dressed as soldiers, kings, and other types of dignitaries. Villagers took satisfaction in having these authoritative figurines perform the menial task of cracking nuts for the more common folk. Today, while some nutcrackers may still crack nuts, most of these colorful figures serve only as decoration.

Whenever we see gingerbread houses, most of us can't help but remember the Grimm's Brothers fairy tale of Hansel and Gretel. In fact, the gingerbread house was used as a decoration in Germany about the same time as the famous story was first published. Interestingly, nobody really knows if the story or the confection came first. However, during the 17th century, gingerbread was a favorite treat throughout Europe, and bakers were protected by bakers' guilds dictating that only they could bake gingerbread, except on Christmas and Easter when it was open to all households.

One German tradition that is not as well-known as those just mentioned, but is equally important to the celebration of Christmas, is *Gemütlichkeit*. When entering many German homes during the holidays, one is often greeted with a warm *"Gemütlichkeit!"* While there is no exact English translation of this word, it roughly means a situation (usually Christmastime) that induces a cheerful mood, peacefulness of mind, social acceptance, and washings of coziness and unhurried leisure.

However, *Gemütlichkeit* is more than just a greeting or saying. It is a state of mind that raptures all of the senses. One feels it through the warmth and love of family and friends. It is seen in the cheery decorations adorning hearth and home. One smells it through the evergreen of the tree and garland or wood smoke from the cozy fire. It is tasted in the sweet and savory flavors of holiday goodies. It is heard from the laughter of merry-makers at an informal Christmas party or through the soft sounds of carolers' songs as they stand around the piano.

It is in the spirit of *Gemütlichkeit* that the true meaning of the word is observed, for this greeting is grounded upon the act of giving rather than receiving. *Gemütlichkeit* is the candle in the window welcoming weary travelers to come and take rest. It is the hope and promise from the words of noted pastor Robert Alden who said, "There is not enough darkness in all the world to put out the light of even one small candle." *Gemütlichkeit* is warmth, happiness, peace, and hope. *Gemütlichkeit* is the pure essence of Christmas all wrapped up into one multi-faceted word.

The Germans gave us a lot of traditions to celebrate and enjoy for our Christmas celebrations. *Gemütlichkeit,* everyone!

###

December 4

Bubble Lights

At some point during my childhood in the 60's, my mother introduced a new type of light to our Christmas tree. The bubble lights she strung across our tree were one of the most amazing spectacles I had ever seen. Up to that time, our tree had white, colored, and even blinking lights. However, this new type of decoration was nothing that I had ever seen before, and the mystery surrounding the bubbles in the glass tube, and how they were made fascinated me greatly.

Bubble lights as Christmas decorations were actually patented back in the 1940's by Carl Otis and introduced by the NOMA Electric Company, one of the largest distributors of Christmas lights at that time. The concept of the bubble light is pretty simple. There is an incandescent bulb encased in a colored plastic covering with a glass tube sticking out of it. The tube was filled with liquid, and when heated by the encased bulb, bubbles would percolate to the top of the tube.

The plastic encasement was multicolored (usually red and green), and the liquid inside the glass tube was amber, red, blue, or green. The liquid was almost always methylene chloride because it had a low boiling point. At the base of the light was a clip to attach it to branches of the tree. Each string usually came with eight bubble lights, and strings could be combined.

Because bubble lights were large and heavy, they were usually attached to the larger branches toward the bottom of the tree. Care also had to be taken to make sure the glass tubes were always upright so that the liquid could be heated by the bulb to activate the bubbles. Even when the lights were attached to the tree in the correct way, the liquid inside sometimes would not bubble. This problem was easily remedied by gently shaking the liquid or by grasping the glass tube with a warm hand.

My mom usually only placed three or four strings of bubble lights on our tree. To me, however, these relatively few lights seemed to make our tree come alive. Not only did the bubbles move rapidly throughout the colored liquid inside the glass tube, this movement was often mirrored as reflections on nearby Christmas ornaments, and it created a rhythmic sparkle to the adjacent metallic garland. Oftentimes when I was by myself or the house was very quiet, I could actually hear the bubbling of the lights.

Sometimes the color from other lights would mingle with the clear liquid and create a whole spectrum of color combinations. Our cats were also amazed at the movement of the bubble lights. Many times they would just sit by the tree observing the movement. Occasionally, one would try to paw at the glass tube. One of our kittens unknowingly tried to jump into the tree after one of the lights. After the tree fell, he didn't try that anymore!

The glass tubes were very rugged and strong and very seldom ever broke. About the only time I ever saw one broken was when we would unpack the lights from their storage boxes kept up in the attic. As with all Christmas lights, however, the bulb would eventually burn out. When that happened, it was impossible to replace just the white bulb in the plastic encasement. One had to buy an entire replacement fixture and screw it into the base of the light string.

As time progressed, the fascination and popularity of this magical decoration grew. Companies soon came out with both smaller and larger sizes of bubble lights. They also made decorative candelabra stands where one bubble light could be screwed into the base and incorporated into flower arrangements, table decorations, or festive fireplace mantles. Later, table decorations were made into snowmen or Santa Clauses that would house one bubble light each. At one point, companies tried adding glitter to the liquid to enhance the bubble effect, but that idea didn't catch on with those of us who were bubble light purists.

Other uses were soon found for the technology behind the bubble lights. A few companies actually tried making Halloween decorations with them using orange and black plastic with orange liquid and incorporating them into Jack-o-lanterns, ghosts, and witches. The methylene chloride liquid was also used in the creation of the Drinking or Dipping Bird, which was another fascinating toy that became popular in the 70's.

Now, with the popularity of synchronized blinking, automatic color changing, low wattage, and cool-to-the-touch technology of LED lights, the bubble light has lost some of its magic and status. However, for those of us who grew up with these fascinating lights as well as many of the younger generation who have grown to appreciate vintage lighting, I believe bubble lights will continue to be a staple on Christmas trees for years to come, still causing young and old alike to admire their rhythmic display and wonder how they actually work.

###

December 5

Christmas at School

Back when I was in grammar school, we could actually celebrate Christmas in the classroom without fear of political retribution, loss of federal and/or state funding, or governmental panic. Back then, the holidays were seen as a happy, joyous time that instilled in students a sense of warmth and caring for their fellow classmates while, at the same time, providing us with a little fun and down time after a tough semester of school work.

Shortly after we returned from Thanksgiving, our teacher brought in a huge, freshly cut evergreen tree for us to decorate. Its fragrance and earthiness permeated our classroom, which usually smelled of chalk, markers, old sneakers, and disinfectant. Because the tree usually came directly from

someone's property nearby, it never was as full or as sym-
metrical as the groomed, store-bought trees were. However,
from the smiles it brought to each one of us, you would have
thought that tree could have hung outside the skating rink at
Rockefeller Center.

During art class, the teacher brought in red and green construction paper with paste glue and glitter. Each of us cut
thin strips from the paper and loop the ends to form a circle.
Then more and more loops were added to form a red and
green Christmas chain that would hang on the tree. After the
chain was built, we worked diligently with paste and glitter
to make the chain sparkle. I still remember the sweet smell of
the paste we used and the fact that I tended to get more glitter
on myself than on the Christmas chain.

Everyone helped drape the long, colorful chain around the
tree. Afterwards, the teacher usually had some glass ornaments and silver icicles to add to the branches. During sub-
sequent art classes, we usually made more ornaments out
of construction paper, cotton, Popsicle sticks, and tempera
paint. By the time we finished the tree, our room looked and
smelled festive and inviting.

Christmas was also used as part of the lesson plan in my
school. During music class, we sang Christmas carols while
the teacher told of each song's origin. During English, we
read stories about Christmas or learned how to write a holiday poem. In math, we learned about multiplication by observing the rows and columns of Christmas cookies on a baking sheet. In Geography, we studied how children all over the
world celebrated the season.

In my class, there was a Jewish boy who was a buddy of mine. The teacher always took some time during Christmas to explain to the class about Hanukkah and the Festival of Lights. She told to us that, instead of celebrating Christmas, the Jewish people celebrated the reclaiming of their holy temple a long time ago. She added that Hanukkah celebrated light over darkness and praised purity and spirituality. When she told us that Jewish children usually received gifts on seven of the eight nights, those of us who celebrated Christmas got a little envious. He always said that he enjoyed participating in all of the fun stuff with his Christian friends.

One year, the teacher gave us a notecard on which we were to write a recipe for almond cookies that she had transcribed on the blackboard. The next day we were given cardboard cones about a foot high. We attached a clothespin to the top of the cone and then sprayed them with gold paint. The cone would serve as a recipe card holder for our mothers while cooking. I thought the idea was pretty ingenious, but I could not wait for mom to cook some of those almond cookies. Before the gift was complete, we were allowed to put some glitter on it. After all, it would not be a school Christmas gift if it were not slathered in glitter.

During this time of year, there was always a Christmas program that was performed in conjunction with the evening PTA meeting that month. We usually had small skits, and we almost always sang Christmas carols. Our principal always dressed up as Santa, but we knew better. The real Santa was fatter than he, and the laughter and talking of this little red elf impostor sounded very similar to the person we knew in the hallways and on the intercom system during the rest of the year.

Right up through my seventh grade year, we even learned Bible verses. In fact, my seventh grade history teacher required us to memorize the first 20 verses of the Christmas story in St. Luke. For extra credit, we could choose to memorize the next 20 verses. Seeing as how I needed all the help I could get, I quickly memorized all 40 verses.

As the last day of class before the holidays wound down, we all wished each other "Merry Christmas" and ardently made sure that we were never caught under the conspicuously placed mistletoe for fear of being kissed by a girl. At the end of the day, many of us gave our teacher a small Christmas gift to show her our appreciation for all the work she had done. Then, we all headed home to begin the holidays with our families. Clearly, when the spirit of Christmas was present in our classroom, it made our lives more enriched and fulfilled. During those years, it was a great time to be a kid.

###

December 6

St. Nicholas Day!

E ach year around December 6th, I celebrate St. Nicholas Day with my staff at the office. Now, most do not know this day exists or the whole story behind it. In fact, when I started doing this little observance, I had to create a little write-up to educate my staff on the importance of this significant day. For me, the day serves to ring in Christmas and provides a unique way to get people in the festive mood for the season. I don't do a lot during this day. I usually give my staff some chocolate, and we all go out to lunch together.

However, Saint Nicholas Day is actually a festival for children in much of Europe related to surviving legends of the saint and, particularly, his reputation as a bearer of gifts. The American Santa Claus, as well as the Anglo-Canadian and

British Father Christmas, derives from these legends. "Santa Claus" is itself derived from the Dutch *Sinterklaas*.

Much of the Saint Nicholas tradition can be traced back to the Germanic god Odin, and his appearance is similar to some portrayals of this god. In the Saint Nicholas tradition in the Netherlands and Flanders (Northern Belgium), he rides a horse over the rooftops, which is similar to Odin's riding through the sky. Also, his assistants, the Zwarte Pieten ('Black Petes'), may be a remnant of the twin ravens that accompanied Odin.

The history of the festive Saint Nicholas celebration is complex and reflects conflicts between Protestantism and Catholicism. You see, Nicholas was a canonized saint. Martin Luther, the great Protestant reformer, replaced the festival that had become associated with the Papacy to a Christkind ("Christ child") celebration on Christmas Eve. The Nicholas celebrations still remain a part of tradition among many Protestants, albeit on a much smaller scale than Christmas. The Protestant Netherlands, however, retain a much larger Saint Nicholas tradition. Many Catholics, on the other hand, have adopted Luther's *Christkind*.

I personally wish that Luther had left this day alone. While I understand his wanting to separate from Catholicism, by moving this celebration to Christmas Eve, I believe he started the diminution of the true meaning of Christmas. He, in effect, transformed the highly significant and holy birth of Jesus to a day when we await a jovial little fat man to deliver gifts to our home. If the original St. Nicholas were still alive today,

I believe he would not want his little ritual to conflict with the Christ Child.

Getting back to the story, in Germany, Nikolaus is usually celebrated on a small scale. Many children put a boot, called *Nikolaus-Stiefel*, outside the front door on the night of December 5 to December 6. St. Nicholas fills the boot with gifts and, at the same time, checks up on the children to see if they were good. If they were not, they will have a tree branch ("Rute") in their boots instead. Sometimes a disguised Nikolaus also visits children at school or in their homes and asks if they have been good: sometimes supposedly checking a book for their record and handing out presents dependent on how good they have been. Like most customs, this practice has become more lenient in recent decades.

But for many children, Nikolaus also elicited fear, as he was often accompanied by Knecht Ruprecht, who threatened to beat or sometimes actually eat the children for misbehavior. Knecht Ruprecht, furthermore, was equipped with goat legs. In Switzerland, where he is called *Schmutzli,* he threatened to put bad children in a sack and take them back to the Black Forest. In other accounts he threw the sack into the river, drowning the naughty children. These traditions were implemented more rigidly in Catholic countries, such as Austria or Bavaria. St. Nicholas was actually a 4th century Catholic Bishop who lived during the time when Christians were being ruthlessly persecuted by Rome. Obeying Jesus' words to "sell what you own and give the money to the poor," Nicholas used his whole inheritance to assist the needy, the sick, and the suffering. Dedicating his life to serving God, he was made Bishop of Myra while still a young man. Bishop Nicholas became known throughout the land for his generosity to those in need and his love for children.

One story of St. Nicholas tells of a poor man with three daughters. In those days, a young woman's father had to offer prospective husbands a dowry. The larger the dowry, the better the chance that a young woman would find a good husband. Without a dowry, a woman was unlikely to marry and was therefore destined to be sold into slavery. Mysteriously, on three different occasions, a bag of gold appeared in their home, providing the needed dowries. The bags of gold, tossed through an open window, are said to have landed in stockings or shoes left before the fire to dry.

Therefore, on December 6th, I celebrate with my office staff the life of a kind and generous person who gave much to others. I do this, in part, to prepare for the more important celebration of the Christ Child who gave His all for us.

###

December 7

A Newborn Christmas

During August of 1997, my wife gave birth to our boy-girl twins. After almost 13 years of marriage, we were at a point where we could finally start a family. With two children at once, however, it seemed we just decided to make up for lost time and go with the two-for-one special. Now, I don't mind saying that I was more than a little nervous at the prospect of being a father. After all, I had never held a baby. I had never changed diapers, bottle-fed, or dressed anyone. I knew that all of this work would be a challenge with one baby. With two, the problem seemed insurmountable.

Well, God gave us healthy babies who, at a very early age, decided that they would sleep all night allowing for mother and father to get a little rest in between the day-to-day routine of almost assembly-line-type work. There was waking and changing. There was feeding and changing. There was napping and changing. There was changing and changing again! After a while, I quickly became a diaper-changing, baby-burping machine.

A few months went by, and the preparations for Christmas were underway. Because of play-pens and other assorted baby paraphernalia around the house, we knew that we could not bring out all of our decorations. However, we put up our tree in the living room just in time for the first snowfall. I set up the village on the buffet table in the dining room. In the den, we put out a few other decorations, and our house was soon dressed for the holiday season.

One night, I was in the living room looking at the tree with my son who was fast asleep in my arms. At that point, the dad role really hit me, and I was able to think beyond diapers, bottles, cribs, and pacifiers. I soon started to reminisce about my childhood and imagine Jay and Jessica with bicycles, toys, stockings, and candy. I then realized that Christmas becomes something significantly more special when children are in the house.

But just as quickly as the thoughts of Christmas with my children came to mind, I looked at the star on our tree, and something else much more profound hit me. I wondered what Joseph must have felt like during that night. To him, Christmas had nothing to do with decorations, presents, or food. For Joseph, it was about seeing the birth of the Christ Child from his wife Mary. It was about his immediate concern for the health and welfare of his new family. After all, when Jesus was born in Bethlehem, his cradle was a manger, and they were residing with farm animals. The smells of livestock, earthiness, and dampness had to bother Joseph who had taken on a huge responsibility.

Like me, most new fathers are filled with nervousness, apprehension, and a fear of the unknown. For me, I remember the time when my wife told me we were having twins. I immediately recalled an article I had read whereby the author stated that parents will spend, on average, about $250,000 from the time their child is born until they marry and move out of the house. I wondered where I could come up with a half a million dollars, and I didn't sleep for three nights. The stress on me was tremendous.

However, I again thought back to Joseph. While I was indeed stressed out, he had the entire world on his shoulders. Not much was written about him. We know he was a carpenter and that he fell in love with Mary. However, Joseph was shocked to find out that his wife-to-be was already pregnant with someone else's child. Back during those days, being pregnant and unwed was a shameful disgrace, and even Joseph had his doubts as to whether he should stay with her.

Then, one night, an angel of the Lord visited Joseph and told him that his soon-to-be wife was still a virgin but that she had a special child inside her.

The angel then told Joseph that he should marry her and help her raise the Son of God. Joseph obeyed, and amid all of the gossip and shunning by many, he raised his family as best as he could. While not specifically mentioned in the Bible, I'm sure that Jesus got much of his physical strength through learning carpentry from his father. I also believed that Jesus' quiet temperament came as much as from Joseph as it did from God. In short, although undocumented, I believe Joseph played a huge role in Jesus' life.

Oftentimes fathers are not given much credit for the work they do in raising their children. Joseph was fully aware of this fact before taking on his huge responsibility. However, it is the steady strength and determination of good fathers that have a lasting influence on the children they raise. Although God was Jesus' father, Joseph was his dad, and Jesus learned much from him.

I settled in my chair with my son in my lap and continued to look at the tree as the snow gently fell outside. While fully aware of the huge task before me as I raised my children as best as I can, I was comforted during Christmas with the thought of Joseph and the huge task he had before him. I looked forward to the many Christmases I would spend with our twins while watching them grow and prosper into what God wants them to be. The job of being a father is tough, but if Joseph was able to do it well with the Son of God, my job now didn't seem so insurmountable.

Thanks, Joseph, for showing all fathers how to be good dads.

###

December 8

The Fireplace at Christmas

There is something very special about having a fireplace during the Christmas season. The warmth and light emitting from the burning logs seem to accentuate the radiance of the holidays to a greater extent and metaphorically symbolize the special warmth that rests in the hearts of most during this sacred time of the year.

Since the dawn of time, fire has served to melt the chill within man's bones, make his fresh kill or catch more palatable to the mouth, harden his hand-formed clay, and ward off vicious creatures with its bright, flickering light. In more recent times, a fire serves more intangible needs than its historic offering of light and heat. It bonds families together around its hearth, becomes a favorite companion to book and beverage, and quickly turns a comfortable room into a quiet, romantic getaway.

More importantly, however, a cozy fire causes man to stop for a while and ponder. As the flickering flames lap up the fuel from the logs feeding it and the red-hot embers hiss and crackle indiscriminately underneath, man finds time to contemplate the long, hard day behind him and prepare for the future that waits. This is the perfect frame of mind to be in during Christmastime when man should always take a moment to ponder his existence in relation to God's perfect gift to mankind.

As a boy, I loved a fire in the fireplace during Christmastime. I remember our Crèche was always placed to the left side of the hearth. While rearranging the cows, sheep, camels, and wise men around the manager, I imagined that our fire was there to warm them all on that cold winter's night.

The fire, however, was not always the sole component of warmth and cheer around that fireplace of ours. During the Christmas season, mom always had the mantel decked out in its special holiday dress. Some years would see colored lights and garland gently draped over it. During others, there would be candles aflame next to strategically placed angel hair and Christmas balls borrowed from the tree. No matter how she fixed it, our mantel always joyously welcomed the season. To this day, I remember the mantel decorations twinkling in dad's eye as he stood and gazed at them and told mom how "cheery" they were.

Now, the mantel was never over decorated. After all, it had to support one of the most important items of the season: the

Christmas stocking. My sister and I usually had two stockings each for all of the fruit, nuts, and candy that were left for us. To this day, an orange or tangerine will always pleasantly take me back to my childhood and Christmas morning. For mom and dad, we found two stockings sewn together and made into a pair of Christmas pants. We even had stockings for our pet cats. To say our mantel was an exhibition during Christmas would be an understatement.

A fire, though, in the fireplace at Christmastime rekindles my memories of hot chocolate and popcorn, the taste of nuts freshly cracked, and their hulls thrown into the fire for added fuel. I'm reminded of Christmas movies watched while in my flannel pajamas and curled up next to my dad in his chair, of our cats lazily sleeping while mom worked in the kitchen baking her famous fruitcake cookies (which were always softer and more delectable than the actual cake from whence they got their name). I especially remember my job of going outside in the cold, frosty air to get fresh logs only to be entranced by the warm, rich, acrid smell of wood smoke from our chimney.

During those Christmases in Florence, Alabama, when it was cold, a fire in the fireplace waited for us as we gathered in the living room of my aunt's house. With so many people in the room exchanging gifts, the heat would be so noticeable that we would oftentimes allow the fire to almost completely extinguish itself. However, after all of the gifts had been given out and the room cleared of the clutter, the adults would let us children gaze into the fire as they placed some of the Christmas wrapping paper inside so that we could see flames of red, purple, yellow, and green as the various inks from the paper ignited.

As I grew older, the Christmas fireplace never lost its charm. I asked my wife to marry me in my parents' basement, which I romantically lit by Christmas tree and firelight. My family now has its own traditions of decorating the mantel and hanging stockings, and I still find solitude and comfort sitting by the fire with a Christmas story or gazing at the bright colored lights on our tree.

As time has progressed, the need for a real fireplace has been replaced by central heat and gas logs. While utilitarian in comfort and convenience, they do little to compare with a real crackling fire in a fireplace at Christmas time: the sight of which takes me back to simpler times and happy memories.

###

December 9

The Balsam Wood Cabin

As a child I noticed that, over the years, my mother added some items to the Christmas village, which was always perched bravely atop the old antique pedestal desk in our living room. Occasionally, she would add a tree or two, create a new pond from a piece of mirror, or include some new figurines of people or animals frolicking in the soft white snow made of cotton and glitter. I remember one year in particular when she ingeniously created a small aluminum foil stream that flowed into the town below from the mountain we made by stacking together atlases and smaller books.

One day a package came, and upon opening it, I discovered mom had bought a real balsam wood log cabin. It was very light weight, about four inches by four inches in size, and it had one door opening in the center with no windows. This cabin fascinated me immensely.

The look, feel, and smell of that log cabin was so woodsy and real that when we placed it on our seemingly artificial village, I quickly imagined the faint call of a lone wolf from within the distant pines, the haunting cry of a loon as he flew gracefully over a dark lake, or the sound of the icy wind as it made its way down to the villagers as they completed their preparations for Christmas.

Every time I looked at that cabin, I thought of fantastic adventures in some far-off wilderness. I easily imagined it to be the modest homestead of Daniel Boone as he helped tame the rugged territory of Kentucky. Through Jack London's *Call of the Wild*, I looked around the cabin to see if Buck the dog was patiently waiting outside for his master to come out and hook up the team.

I remembered my English teacher a few months before reading excerpts from Henry David Thoreau, and I thought of his cabin on Walden Pond along with this passage: "A lake is the landscape's most beautiful and expressive feature. It is Earth's eye; looking into which the beholder measures the depth of his own nature." I picked the cabin up from its original location and placed it by the large mirrored lake toward the left front side of the village and waited for ole Henry to come out of his warm cabin to fish for his dinner.

Now, there was something very special about that log cabin. The roof could be removed, and a burner with incense could be placed inside and lighted. The cabin came with a package of 12 incense cones that smelled of evergreen; and it took only a few seconds for that heavenly aroma to fill the entire living room.

The true magic of the cabin was soon realized when the incense was ignited and the roof was placed back on the structure. In a second or so, smoke would rise up from its chimney and hover over the little village. From that point forward, Christmas would never be complete without the smell of evergreen incense and little puffs of white smoke billowing from the chimney of the little cabin.

As the years progressed, our Christmas village got more elaborate and fancy. New porcelain homes replaced the tired, tattered cardboard ones. Plastic snow replaced the cotton, and new lighting technology allowed for more creativity. However, I always made sure that our balsam wood cabin was placed next to the big mirror pond, to the left of the town, where its smoke and its memories could be enjoyed by all.

My mom doesn't put up the village anymore, and that old balsam wood cabin is forever packed away in a box much like its memory is tucked gently in my mind until the smell of evergreen incense burning somewhere awakens it to full glory. Maybe I need to rescue that old cabin from the Christmas box and rekindle the smell of holidays past when a small house of wood ignited the imagination of a young boy at Christmastime.

Note: This story was originally published in the Christmas, 2016 edition of Ideals Magazine.

December 10

The Aromas of Christmas

While it is true that Christmas entices all of the senses of hearing, sight, touch, smell, and taste, its effect on smell is probably more complex and satisfying than with any of our other senses. After all, Christmas is a time when smells are abundant in variety and plentiful in presence. One cannot go into a house or business during the holiday season without distinctively smelling Christmas. One cannot walk outside in the snow-covered wood or take a stroll down a busy city street without being rewarded by the pleasant aromas of yuletide fare.

One of the first aromas of the season is the smell of fresh cut evergreen. During those years when my family bought a real tree, the smell of it permeated the house. Long before the Christ Child was born, evergreen was brought into homes in the middle of winter in anticipation of spring and the promise of lush green all over the countryside.

Cinnamon and clove are also a common fragrances of Christmas. They are used in baking, on boiled custard, and inside decorative straw brooms hung around the house. Cinnamon and clove have a warm, cozy aroma that rekindles memories of when I helped my grandmother in the kitchen as she prepared all of the goodies for our Christmas feast. Both are also used in potpourri, and their soothing tastes are a welcomed addition to apple cider or coffee.

What would Christmas be without the smell of baking? When I was a child, some of my first recollections of the holidays were the heavenly aromas coming from the oven as mom baked her seven layer cookies. This fragrance was a treat reserved only for Christmas, and just as the smell of baked sweet potatoes welcomes fall and Thanksgiving, the aroma of mom's seven layer cookies welcomed Christmas. It was a treat to smell the graham cracker, butterscotch, chocolate, coconut, and sweetened condensed milk slowly baking in the oven.

Mom also baked her fruitcake cookies. These were actually eaten, unlike the traditional fruitcakes that were given as gifts, only to be used as doorstops throughout the year. As a boy, mom would let me help her put the nuts with red and green candied fruit into the batter. She would then let me spoon out the completed dough onto baking sheets. I always noticed how the uncooked batter had a pleasant, but completely different smell to it than the finished baked cookie.

When I got married and visited my wife's house during the holidays, my mother-in-law would be always baking or cooking something that smelled great. She was known all over Tuscaloosa County for her friendship cakes, hand-dipped chocolate coconut candy, and tea cake cookies. The scents of her baking were complemented by the exotic aroma of coffee brewing over on the back counter. I always felt that I gained ten pounds just by smelling what she was baking during the holidays.

Other smells that, to me, are equally important during the holidays are those that are outside. The smell of the frosty night air with the occasional whiff of cows or horses grazing nearby tends to scourer out my lungs and reminds me of the first scents that the Christ child smelled while he was laying in the manger. The acrid, sweet-sour smell of wood smoke wafting over the rooftops of houses nearby is a fragrance that has been around for thousands of years as man made his living space more comfortable and his food more palatable through the use of fire.

One of the smells that I love came in our stockings, without fail, every Christmas morning. As we poured out the contents of our stockings on the floor, I was happy to see brightly colored oranges and tangerines. I loved the clean, citrus smell that seemed to contrast with all of the other smells of the season. When tarted to peel one of the fruits, the fragrant oils released into the air and onto my hands, making the aroma of that experience last long after the fruit had been eaten.

There was also the smell of chocolate and nuts around our home on Christmas. I still enjoy opening the red, green, or silver foil from around a chocolate Kiss. The cocoa smell hit my nose seconds before the taste of the candy hit my mouth. In our stockings was also an assortment of nuts. There were pecans, walnuts, Brazil nuts, and hazelnuts. Cracking open the small treats with a hand-held nut cracker released earthy aromas into the air.

As Christmas dinner was cooking, there were numerous aromas competing for attention in the kitchen. The roasted turkey in the oven mingled nicely with the sage and onion of mom's delectable cornbread dressing. Potatoes boiling in the pan had a clean, earthy aroma to them while the smells of baked bread, cranberries, and pumpkin pie bade welcome to watering mouths. Then the whiffs of fresh roasted coffee and the fruity aroma of chilled Riesling rounded out the smells of Christmas in our kitchen.

To me, another important smell of Christmas is the smell of candles burning. From the dinners at my grandmother's, to the meals we ate at my parents' house, candles were always used during the holidays. Candles decorated our house and the windows of our church. At the end of the Christmas night service, candles were usually lighted as the lights in the church were dimmed and the congregation began to sing *Silent Night*. Afterwards, as we extinguished each candle, the aroma always reminded me of the smell of candles being blown out on a birthday cake. I would leave the church with the warm feeling that, on Christmas Day, we would all be celebrating the most important birthday of all.

###

December 11

The Color Wheel Tree

Recently, while browsing an antique store, I came across a silver aluminum Christmas tree complete with the revolving color wheel that stood on the floor next to it. Looking at the combo, I smiled and remembered a time when Christmas got caught between the forces of technology and commercialism. I also remember my friend Matt's house.

During the holidays, many years ago, Matt and I had been riding our bikes around the neighborhood, and we stopped at his house for some refreshment. When I walked into his house, I saw a very odd sight. It was a six-foot tall Christmas tree unlike anything I had ever seen. Instead of evergreen, this tree was completely silver. Matt's mother had decorated it with red, green, and blue ornaments and it seemed like a very modern contraption sitting in their living room.

That same year, my mom had bought a real tree and had it frocked to make it look like snow was on its branches. I remember the aroma of a real tree in our house. It smelled earthy, spicy, and warm. This new metal tree had no aroma, and it certainly didn't seem exhibit any warmth.

However, to get the full effect of the aluminum tree, one had to see it at night. An electronic wheel that stood low beside the tree was plugged into the wall. Next to the base of the wheel was a bright flood light. In front of the light was a plastic wheel that was separated into colors – usually four to six – and, as the wheel turned, the white light from the bulb was filtered through the wheel, making the tree seem like it was magically changing colors.

While I knew that the tree had the same decorations on it, every time it changed color, the tree seemed to take on a new and unique look. Sometimes, I would briefly argue with myself as to which color was best. To me, the yellow and green light seemed to warm up the tree a little while the blue and red light seemed to increase its richness and definition. There were a few people who decided to just use a white light on the tree, accenting it with either monochromatic or contrasting colored decorations.

So, what caused a contraption like the aluminum Christmas tree to be invented? What led to its demise? Back in 1957, the Soviets launched the first man-made satellite into orbit around the Earth. Sputnik, as it was called, was a polished metal sphere that single-handedly launched the US into the space race. Metals, plastics, and electronics soon became synonymous with high technology, and it seemed like everything that was being manufactured had a sterile, minimalist, futuristic flare to it.

As the story goes, the aluminum Christmas tree got started in Manitowoc, Wisconsin, in 1959 by the Aluminum Specialty Company. Beforehand, the company had made canteens during World War II and, afterwards, was renowned for making toys and boats. Tom Gannon, a toy sales manager, saw a metallic tree in a storefront window in Chicago. He thought the tree looked futuristic, and he took the idea back to his company where they mass produced it and made it affordable. During its year, the company literally sold hundreds of thousands of the tinsel trees ranging from a small table-top model to a giant eight footer.

So, from 1959 to about 1965, the "Evergleam" became the tree of choice for many American homes, and soon, one could take an evening drive down any subdivision or city street and see aluminum Christmas trees in many homes and businesses rhythmically changing color from red, blue, yellow, and green. I remember asking my dad why lights could not be attached to the tree like way we decorated our live one at home. Dad told me that such a move could cause an electrical short and create a fire.

Strangely enough, the demise of this metallic wonder was brought about by none other than the cartoon figure Charlie Brown. In the popular television special *Merry Christmas, Charlie Brown*, Lucy asks Charlie Brown to get a "..big bright shiny aluminum Christmas tree...maybe one painted pink."

Charlie Brown and his friend Linus decide to purchase a real tree because, as they said, Christmas had become too commercial.

Soon, aluminum Christmas trees stood for everything that was wrong with Christmas. By and by, whether people fought to overcome the commercialism of the season or to add warmth to a sterile, technological world, the metallic trees waned as the 60's came to a close.

Now, the aluminum Christmas tree is seeing a resurgence. Today the shiny tree is not seen as a symbol of commercialism. Rather, it is an icon of the 60's along with the transistor radio, instamatic cameras, and plastic furniture. However, today this icon can cost hundreds of dollars rather than the $25 it originally cost. I wasn't too fond of them during their heyday. Now, I smile when I see one. Furthermore, my daughter thinks they are cool.

###

December 12

Christian Symbolism in Dickens' *A Christmas Carol*

Many years ago when I was in my 20's, I attended a service at my church during the Christmas season. During the sermon, the preacher told the congregation that he had gotten into the habit of reading Charles Dickens' *A Christmas Carol* during the holidays. He continued to say that, in fact, he had read it every year for the past 15 years. This claim puzzled me. I wondered why anyone would want to read the same book over and over again. I then recollected how my wife tends to hassle me because I watch the same old Christmas movies year after year. Maybe I'm no different than my pastor.

While I was familiar with *A Christmas Carol*, I had to confess that I had never read the book. I had watched many movie versions of the tale and determined that the 1951 version with Alastair Sim was the best of them all. I had also seen the Donald Duck and "The Muppets" version and remembered seeing it as a locally performed play years ago. I just never took the opportunity to actually pick up the original book and read it. As I left that church service, I decided that I would give it a try.

My first surprise was how short the book actually was. It was one hundred pages. If you had to read Dickens in high school like I did, you will know that his books are much longer than that. Actually, Dickens published many novels, short stories, plays, and non-fiction books. *David Copperfield* was considered his most autobiographical work because, at the age of ten, he was forced to work in a factory to pay off his father's debts.

As to his little Christmas story, *A Christmas Carol* was one of the fastest published classics. Dickens began writing it in October of 1843, and it was published that same year on December 17th. The first printing of 6,000 copies sold out in days, and since its original publication, it has never been out of print. So, with book in hand, I started to read. I loved it. Now, like my pastor, I read it every Christmas season. After a few years of reading it, however, I was soon struck at how much Christian symbolism is in the story. While some of it is obvious, most of the symbolism requires a little thought.

To begin with, a synopsis of the story reveals that Ebenezer Scrooge is a greedy, hateful, covetous sinner who seems to be beyond help. On Christmas Eve, Scrooge is visited by the ghost of his partner who died seven years ago. He is also visited by the three ghosts of Christmases Past, Present, and Yet to Come who show him his sinful ways. Scrooge decides to change his life. On Christmas Day, Scrooge is re-born and promises to "keep Christmas in my heart the whole year."

Now, Scrooge's movement from selfishness to compassion is something that everyone responds to on a positive level. In the Bible, the Gospel parallels this story because there are many instances where people made the decision to transform their lives for the better in keeping with the spirit of Christ.

It is interesting to note that when Dickens came up with the title for his book, he could have called it anything he wanted such as *A Christmas Ghost Story* or just *A Christmas Story*. Instead, he called it *A Christmas Carol*. In today's world, a "carol" can mean anything from "Deck the Halls" to "Jingle Bells." However, during Dickens' time, the term carol was used only for songs celebrating the birth of Jesus Christ. Furthermore, to enhance the significance of his title, Dickens used the musical term "stave," which are stanzas in a song, rather than "chapter" to separate sections of the book.

Throughout the story, there are lights everywhere. Specifically, Dickens often used the contrast of the dark, cold, gloomy streets of London to the brightly lighted shops and homes where people gathered to celebrate the season. Light, especially in its relationship to darkness, is frequently mentioned in the Bible. Job, 23:28, declares "He redeemed my soul from going down to the pit, and I will live to enjoy the light." Jesus sates in John, 9:5, that "While I am in the world, I am the light of the world." In Psalm, 39: 15, we read, "Blessed are those who have learned to acclaim you, who walk in the light of your presence, O Lord." There are many more examples of how light is used in the Bible.

Scrooge, however, believed that darkness was cheap and good. While sitting by his meager fire in his house eating his gruel, he faces a fireplace that has numerous tiles surrounding it depicting dozens of Bible stories. However, the light from the fire is so dim, Scrooge does not notice them. Clearly Scrooge was full of hate, greed, and darkness. In Mark, 8:36, Jesus tells us "What good is it for a man to gain the whole world, yet forfeit his soul?"

The number seven is also seen in *A Christmas Carol* and in the Bible many times. Originally, Dickens wrote that Marley had died ten years ago. He later changed it to "seven years ago, this very night." The number seven is mentioned seven times in connection to the death of Marley, the worldly miser turned divine messenger to Scrooge. The number seven is mentioned in the Bible 860 times. In Genesis, God created the earth in seven days. The Bible also states that seven is a holy number that symbolizes completeness.

The Bible, as a whole, was originally divided into seven major divisions including the Law, the Prophets, the Gospels, Acts, the General Epistles, the Epistles of Paul, and the Book of Revelation. The total number of originally inspired books was 49, or 7x7, demonstrating the absolute perfection of the Word of God. In the Book of Revelation, there are seven churches, seven angels to the seven churches, seven seals, seven trumpet plagues, seven thunders, and the seven last plagues. Moreover, the first resurrection of the dead takes place at the seventh trumpet, completing salvation for the Church.

When it comes to Marley, a good bit of symbolism surrounds him. When he visited Scrooge, he was a transparent specter. In fact, Scrooge believed it might prove an embarrassment to his old partner if he was asked to sit down, seeing that his former partner might fall through the chair. Dickens wrote "Scrooge had often heard it said that Marley had no bowels, but he had never believed it until now." In the Bible, 1 John mentions the "bowels of compassion." Here, Dickens may be referring to Marley's lack of compassion and the reason for his eternal damnation. In fact, Marley died on Christmas Eve. Christ was born on Christmas Day. Thus, symbolically, Marley never knew Christ.

Scrooge was soon visited by the Ghost of Christ Past. He was described as a kind, fatherly figure with a light shining around him. He took Scrooge to visit places of his past. The ghost tells Scrooge that he will be viewing shadows from the past and that neither Scrooge nor the ghost can be seen. In Ecclesiastes, 3:15, we read "Whatever is has already been, and what will be has been before; and God will call the past into account." When they returned to Scrooge's house, the light emitting from the ghost's head was so bright that Scrooge wanted to extinguish it by pulling the ghost's cap further over his head. In Luke, 11:34, we read "your eye is the lamp of your body. When your eyes are good, your whole body also is full of light. But when they are bad, your body also is full of darkness. See to it, then, that the light within you is not darkness." The next ghost to visit Scrooge was the Ghost of Christmas

Present. Scrooge was surprised to see him in his sitting room, the fire blazing in his fireplace, and the spirit sitting on a throne made of food and drink. This specter was a joyous creature who took Scrooge around London to show him how people young and old, rich or poor, celebrated the holidays. Here, the ghost was trying to convey to Scrooge the abundance of life when one walks with the Lord. In John, 10:10, Jesus says "I have come that they may have life, and have it more abundantly." In 1 Thessalonians, 5:9, we learn "For God did not appoint us to suffer wrath but to receive salvation through our Lord Jesus Christ."

Toward the end of their journey, Scrooge noticed that there were two horrible looking children clutching to the legs of the spirit under his robe. "This Boy is Ignorance and the Girl is Want," said the ghost. "Beware them both, and all of their degree, but most of all beware this boy, for on his brow I see that written which is Doom, unless the writing be erased." On ignorance, Jesus says in John, 14:6, that "I am the way, and the truth, and the life. No one comes to the Father except through me." On want, 1 Timothy, 6:10, tells us that "For the love of money is the root of all evil which while some coveted after, they have erred from the faith, and pierced themselves through with many sorrows."

When Scrooge was visited by the Ghost of Christmas Yet to Come, he was more fearful than he had ever been. The ghost made him see unpleasant visions that would happen if Scrooge did not change his ways. In 2 Corinthians, 7:10, we read that "Godly sorrow brings repentance that leads to salvation and leaves no regret, but worldly sorrow brings death."

In Ezekiel, 18:30, we are told to "Repent! And turn from all your transgressions, so iniquity will not be your ruin."

Now, Bob Cratchit was Scrooge's clerk, and Scrooge treated him horribly. However, even though he had a large family to support and very little money to help him with that task, Bob was always a man of kind demeanor who always welcomed Christmas and the joy it brought to him. In essence, Cratchit symbolizes Matthew, 5:3-5, which is referred to as the Beatitudes or the "Sermon on the Mount." This is where Christ said "Blessed are the poor in spirit: for theirs is the kingdom of Heaven; they that mourn: for they shall be comforted; the meek: for they shall inherit the earth..."

It is also interesting to note that there is symbolism in Cratchit's last name. In using it, Dickens used the root word "cratch," which is the English cockney word for *Crèche*, or the Manger of the baby Jesus. Now, Bob also had a young crippled son named Tiny Tim. Scrooge would later find out from the spirits that little Tim would not survive if something was not done to help him. In the book, Bob tells his wife what happened when he and the boy came home from church. "He told me, coming home, that he hoped the people saw him in the church, because he was a cripple, and it might be pleasant to them to remember upon Christmas Day, who made lame beggars walk, and blind men see."

Food is also mentioned many times in the book. In fact, it is very difficult to read it if one is hungry because the wonderful way Dickens describes food. In Psalm, 34:8, we read "Oh, taste and see that the Lord is good: Blessed is the man who takes refuge in him." We also find in Acts, 27:35, "And when he had said these things, he took bread, and giving thanks to God in the presence of all, he broke it and began to eat."

Even Scrooge's first name, "Ebenezer" has a Christian meaning. In 1 Samuel, the Ebenezer is identified with a particular site, about four miles south of Gilgal, where the Israelites were twice defeated by the Philistines and the Ark of the Covenant was stolen. The site wasn't named Ebenezer until after the Israelites finally defeated the Philistines, and took back the Ark. To commemorate the victorious battle, Samuel set up a marker-stone and named it Ebenezer or "stone of help." Here, Dickens may be trying to use Scrooge as a helpful sign to others to show that anyone can turn his or her life around by following Christ.

Probably the most significant feature in *A Christmas Carol* to hit me as strong symbolism of Christianity was the depiction of the spirits themselves. Here we have the Ghost of Christmas Past, the Ghost of Christmas Present, and the Ghost of Christmas Yet to Come. In Revelation, 1:19, we read "Write these things which you have seen, and the things which are, and the things which will take place after this." However, to me, the most powerful meaning behind these ghosts is that they seem to symbolize the Trinity which is God, the Father; God, the Son, and God, the Holy Ghost.

Whether you agree with me about the Christian symbolism or not, *A Christmas Carol* should definitely be on your reading list during the Christmas holidays.

###

December 13

Gift Giving

Right after the flame of the Jack-o-Lantern candle extinguishes Halloween, I start to think about Christmas gifts. Now, mind you, I am not thinking of what I want from my wife, family, and friends. Rather, I am eagerly thinking of what I what I'm going to get them. I can't really explain it, but I start to feel childlike and playful when deciding on the gifts that I want to give. To me, this moment is one of the most enjoyable endeavors during Christmas, and my innocent, adolescent actions give veneration to the One whose birthday we celebrate.

I'm not saying that I don't like to receive gifts. Who doesn't? I really like the anticipation of seeing a gift with my name on it under the tree and letting my mind wonder on all kinds of things that may be inside the nicely wrapped box. In most cases, the anticipation is more exciting than the actual gift itself. I guess it has to do with the fact that someone thought enough about me to find something special and offer it wrapped with care and love.

For me, however, giving a gift to someone I care about beats, hands down, receiving a gift. When thoughts of football and Thanksgiving fill most people's minds, mine is actively plotting and scheming what to get, how to get it, and how to wrap it. Each of these steps has special delicious challenges and obstacles, and each step has to be strategically planned and perfectly executed.

Deciding on the right gift is the first challenge. I try to recall anything that was said by the recipient earlier that year that could prompt me to a great gift choice. I think back to something we did that year or something that happened that may provide the perfect opportunity. I believe a gift should tell something special to the receiver. Christmas is not the time to give a generic gift or to try to flatter with expense. In fact, some of the most precious gifts you can give someone are not extravagant. They are personal. They are you. If I am lucky, I would have found the perfect gift during one of my earlier business trips that I could buy miles away from the recipient. My quest leads to the next challenge of getting the gift. For me, I can't just go into a store and purchase it. Someone, undoubtedly, will see me and spoil the surprise. I have to think stealthily when actually getting the gift. This is when I can ask my friends to get it for me, or order it from far away only to have it shipped and hidden in my office at work, or (even more crafty) to purchase it myself and hide it in that obvious place where the recipient would never dream of looking. All of these are great ideas.

Presenting the gift is also a challenge. It never fails that when I try to wrap the gift at home, the recipient suddenly appears, and I have to quickly hide it or be foiled forever. And while I may have the gift of words to communicate; of numbers to analyze; and skills to garden, repair, or build; I sincerely believe the good Lord forgot to give me the gift of gift wrapping. My wrapped gifts tend to look like tortured souls in straitjackets trying to escape. I comfort myself with the fact that it is the thought that counts as I try to place the twelfth piece of tape over that one stubborn, uneven corner that won't stay where it should. When all of the gifts are placed under the tree, everyone can tell the ones that I have wrapped, and I soon become the focus of some brief Christmas humor. I don't care; however, I have achieved my quest and the gift challenge is complete.

Now, I usually don't spend a lot of money on gifts. One doesn't need to. One of the nicest gifts I have been given was home-baked goods from close friends of ours. I will always remember them every time I bite into a pecan tort. Some of the gifts I have made. One year I gave framed pictures of photos I had taken during my travels. The purpose of giving a gift is to also give something personal of yourself.

Unfortunately, the joy, pleasure, and excitement of gift giving have today been neutered by the sterile and oh-so generic gift card. Whoever came up with this idea never experienced the joy of true gift giving. With the gift card, you might as well greet each other on Christmas Day with a ten spot in your hands, only to quickly exchange them. What is the joy in that? How impersonal and cold that is.

Just when I thought that all hope is gone and gift giving has become innocuous and mechanical, I see that my daughter has got her dad's same mischievous eye, sneaky personality, and tireless tenacity to plan hours finding that perfect gift. I smile because I know that true gift giving may not be lost forever.

###

December 14

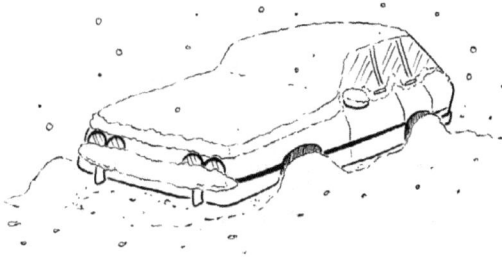

A Southern Snowstorm – Part 1

The snowstorm of 1963, which hit parts of the south during that winter, would not have been such a big deal a few hours drive north of us. After all, a foot or less of snow up there is but a mere inconvenience. However, that year the northwestern wind came down south with a vengeance and froze Memphis with single-digit temperatures, while moisture from the Gulf hung thick in the southern valleys, mountains, and open fields that lay barren from autumn's harvest. When the two systems collided, a southern snowstorm was the result. Although I was very young, I still remember it vividly.

For parts of Tennessee and Alabama, the winter wonderland clogged highways and streets, choked cities and towns, and incapacitated the region's residents. Unlike its northern neighbors, the south was unprepared for such rare weather. It had very little salt to spread on bridges and virtually no snowplows to clear roads and highways. In Knoxville, Tennessee, where we lived, eight inches fell, taking everyone by surprise. That snowfall was the first one I remember and one of the largest since.

I recall little about life or the Christmases we had in Knoxville during the short time we lived there. After all, I was just four years old. I do remember our Christmas trees were real, and their aroma permeated the house. I remember mom starting a tradition of stringing popcorn for our tree. However, the year before, I ate more than I strung, and I got very sick. From that point on, I don't remember mom ever wanting to string popcorn again.

However, this particular Christmas in 1963 was unforgettable in two distinct ways. First, the country was coming to grips with an incredible loss: one that a young boy like myself could not quite fully understand. Second, during all of this national turmoil and uncertainty, a small event happened in my family's little world – insignificant by most people's standards – but it changed my life for the better because I would come to learn something important and enduring about Christmas. As a young boy, I was anticipating all the wonderful things that Christmas usually brings to a child. It was two days before Christmas, and my family was preparing to travel down to Florence, Alabama to spend the holiday with my grandmother and the rest of my dad's family. Just a few weeks beforehand, President Kennedy had been assassinated, and the country was in shock. Therefore, it was comforting and reassuring for families all over the country, who were filled with anxiety and mourning, to come together for the holidays that year.

It was evening on the 23rd, and I was in the living room in our home in Knoxville gazing at our pretty Christmas tree while listening to the festive music of Perry Como, Mitch Miller, Walter Brennen, and more of my parents' favorite songs coming from the stereo. The room smelled of mom's seven-layer cookies as she pulled them out of the oven. The intoxicating aromas of chocolate, butterscotch, coconut, and pecans competed with and teased my taste buds in an oh-so delectable way. Occasionally, I would look out of the window at the colored lights adorning the doors and windows of neighboring houses. The heart-warming lights bravely shined against the cold, dark skies of a wintry Tennessee December evening.

Mom, dad, and my sister were finishing up wrapping the many gifts we would take to Florence. Being only four, I was too young for this endeavor, and I eagerly awaited the time when I would be older so that I, too, could sit at the table and engage in such important-looking work. I distinctly remember my mom and dad making sure that all of the gifts had the right card attached to them. My mom wanted to make sure that the warm hat intended for my balding uncle Charlie would not be mistakenly given to my aunt or that my grandmother's flannel nightgown would not wind up in the lap of my cousin Blair.

"They say we're going to have some snow tomorrow," my mom said as she checked off gifts from her list and leaned over the dining room table to grab some ribbon for the package she had just wrapped. "I hope it will not be too much. We have a long drive ahead of us tomorrow."

My dad, who had just gotten up from his chair to stuff one of the warm seven-layer cookies into his mouth, chewed out his reply "Me too, Clara."

He then took a drink of his Diet Dr. Pepper from his glass that had been frosted by the freezer and parroted her concern "We do have a long drive tomorrow." Later on in life, I always wondered if my dad thought that a diet drink would somehow cancel out the calories of a huge dinner or one of mom's desserts. I know it never worked for me.

Lying on the living room floor that evening, I was lost in thought and imagination as the sights, smells, and sounds of Christmas surrounded me. I was not yet aware that the cookies were cool enough to be eaten. Instead, I wondered what Santa would bring me and if the weather would be better on Christmas Day so that I could go out and play. My mouth also watered and my lips smacked in anticipation at the candy and goodies I would get in my stocking hung conspicuously by the fireplace.

Looking back on those days, I now realize that my excitement came more from the anticipation of Christmas rather than the actual day itself. While I always loved and honored the day, it was my youthful wonderment, anticipation, and imagination leading up to Christmas that made those times seem a lot sweeter. Suddenly, however, a cold chill ran down my spine, and my childish mind begin to worry.

"Mom, is our chimney big enough for Santa?"

Mom looked up at me from one of the packages she was wrapping. "It is more than large enough," she answered with a laugh.

I was not convinced, "How can he come down the Chimney when a fire is burning? Won't he get burned?"

My frightening scenarios would soon be pacified as mom reassured me in a calming voice "Why, Drew, he is Santa. He can do anything."

Her words were as comforting to me as the taste of the cookies I just discovered and washed down with ice cold milk. However, her words as well as her cookies barely had time to settle inside me when I heard her voice again.

"Time to go to bed, Drew," she said with excitement.

Well, there was nothing exciting to me about those words. I loved everything about Christmas and didn't want to leave it. Then mom bent down to where I was in the kitchen, kissed my cheek, and blotted some of the cookie and milk from my mouth.

"Remember, tomorrow we have to get up early to go to Florence."

Well, that was the only encouragement I needed as I ran into my room. All the time I was thinking that tomorrow would be an exciting day of travel, of adventures, and, best of all, of grandmother's house. I crawled into the bed, pulled the warm covers snuggly to my chin, and went to sleep soundly.

The next morning I awoke to the smell of bacon in the house and my sister, who is four years older than me, running all over the house exclaiming that there was snow outside. It looked like our family would have our first white Christmas that I could remember! I rubbed my eyes and quickly got out of bed. As I opened the curtain to my window, I could barely see outside for the frost that had congealed on the panes.

The weather was uncharacteristically cold and snowy during that Christmas Eve morning.

Looking out on the lawn from my bedroom window, I was amazed to see all the snow that had accumulated the night before. I hurriedly put on my robe and slippers and made my way for the living room. I wanted to see our Christmas tree set against a real background of snow, and I didn't want it all to melt before I got there. I ran as fast as I could down the hall in what mom said sounded like a herd of elephants charging. From our living room window, I noticed the day seemed brighter with the sunlight reflecting upon the thick blanket of white snow. Deep furrows were cut into the white roadway from the occasional passing vehicle. The gentle snowdrifts with their frothy peaks reminded me of meringue on my favorite pie, and the deep clear blue sky contrasted nicely with the white, winter wonderland below it.

There wasn't enough time, though, to gaze outdoors. My family was packing to go to Florence to spend Christmas at my grandmother's.

"Hurry to breakfast before it gets cold, Drew" mom called out from the kitchen. "We have to hurry so that we can leave early. We have a long way to go and there is so much snow outside."

I quickly ate my breakfast and drank my hot chocolate. I

stealthily looked around the kitchen for some of mom's seven layer cookies, but none could be found.

It then occurred to me that we would be leaving our house. While I was excited about the road trip through the snow, the terrifying reality of what was about to happen finally set in my young brain. We were leaving our house on Christmas Eve! Would Santa know where we had gone? Would he follow us, or would he just leave our toys here for our return? The thought of that notion filled me with dread.

"Wait, mom," I said with terror in my voice. "We will not be here when Santa comes. How will he know where we are?"

Mom patted me on the head, "Drew, remember I told you that Santa can do anything. You just have to believe."

I heard what mom said, but all I could believe at that moment was the fact that I would be waking up on Christmas morning at grandmother's with no toys. To a four-year-old, that thought was almost too much to bear, and it stayed with me while my parents packed the car and got ready for the trip. Soon, mom was helping me with my coat and ear muffs. She clearly saw the concern in my eyes.

"Don't worry, Drew. Santa will know where we are."

Before I could contemplate her words, dad opened our garage door, and the icy wind invaded our warm, cozy home. I knew we were about to leave. As I headed outside, I felt the wind tighten the skin on my cheeks and turn my small nose red. The weather outside was shockingly cold, but exhilarating at the same time. I shivered a little, and I could feel the blood racing though my body. The cold air was fresh, clean, and spiced with wood smoke from nearby chimneys. From that point on, the pungent smell of smoke on a frosty day harkens me back to that morning and intimately connects me to the Christmas season.

I remember the snow crunching beneath my feet as I walked out to our blue Chevrolet with my sister and mom. I never remembered walking on snow before. It was an awkward feeling. Mom told us that dad would follow behind us in his old Hilman. This plan seemed strange to me because we always traveled in one car as a family. I turned to dad and looked at him as he was scrapping snow off of his windshield.

"Dad, why are you not going with us?"

Dad stopped his work for a moment and bent down toward me. "Well, Drew, you saw all of the presents we have for everyone." He walked me around to the back of his car and waved over the massive pile of presents inside. "We cannot fit all of the presents and all of us in one car."

What dad said made sense. However, I hated the thought of him riding alone.

"Dad, why don't I ride with you?"

Dad patted me on my back and smiled, "Well, Drew, that would be great, but mom said she wanted a man in the car with her, and seeing how I have to drive this car, you are the best candidate."

After hearing those words, I felt a little bigger as I crawled into the front seat of the Chevrolet and we drove off into the morning's icy coldness. My body in the front seat was so small that my head barely peaked over the dashboard. However, I sat

up straight as an arrow and looked out over the snowy vast-
ness while mom drove carefully down the road. Dad had just
appointed me her protector, and I now had the responsibility
to make sure I did my job well.

On a good day, the trip from Knoxville to Florence would
be over five hours. On this day, it took us eight. There was
snow everywhere. The frost congealed on the windows and
windshield of our car while we followed the long, slow line of
trucks and cars ahead of us. The trip seemed to take forever,
and mom seemed more nervous behind the wheel than usual. There were policemen at various locations waving their
hands, shouting at other vehicles, and pointing the way with
their flashlights. Looking out at them, I saw they were doing
an important job. For a moment, I wanted to be a policeman.

To keep my sister and I entertained through the long trip, my
mom got both of us to tell what we had asked Santa for Christmas. We then started talking about the food that would be at
grandmother's house when we all sat down to eat on Christmas Day. As the car moved forward, I envisioned grandmother's table covered in turkey and dressing, mashed potatoes, rolls, corn, beans, as well as the latest casserole dishes
that came from *Good Housekeeping* magazine with the promise
that they would be the hit at the party. To me, however, nothing could be better than simple turkey and dressing covered
in piping hot gravy.

On grandmother's sideboard would be the desserts. There
were pies, cakes, cookies, along with red and green Jell-O
molds with marshmallows inside. One of my favorites was
my aunt Biddy's chocolate pound cake. It was so moist and

chocolaty that it quickly melted in my mouth with each fork-ful. Along with the food were the table decorations. There were candles and holly with an occasional Santa Clause or reindeer hiding behind the butter or the cranberry sauce. The anticipation of that wonderful table with all of its goodness made me smile as we passed by other families going into the homes of other grandmothers who, I thought, probably had wonderful tables like ours waiting for them.

Occasionally, I would snap back to reality and look back to see if dad was still behind us. He was. I continued to concentrate on my job as protector of mom. Dad gave me that important job, and I was intent on its purpose, although I was not really sure what to do. The car was very warm inside as compared to the bitter cold that was apparent on the breaths of the peo-ple who were outside with their cars stuck in the snow or the exhaust billowing from the tailpipes of the various automo-biles all around us. Mom also had the wipers turned on to move the snow from the windshield and to clear the incessant frost forming on it. The rhythmic sound of the wipers and the warmth of the car were too much for a young boy, and soon I fell fast to sleep.

I don't remember passing through Chattanooga or crossing the Alabama state line. I do remember driving past Hunts-ville. At one point, a few cars pulled in front of my dad who was behind us, and soon, we lost track of where he was. Mom wanted to pull over, but there was no room for her to do so. Only one lane was moving, and we were in it. It was like we were hooked to all of the cars in front and behind us like one, large, slow-moving train, and we could not obstruct it on its journey by stopping or trying to pull to the side. Dad surely was just a few cars behind us. But we didn't really know where he was.

As we moved forward, the sun was setting in the western sky with its warm glow reflecting on the snowy hills and countryside of north Alabama. Part of me looked around in wonder and amazement while another part of me constantly looked back in hopes of catching a glimpse of dad's Hilman. It was not to be found. Moving onward, the sun disappeared below the horizon, and we were enveloped in an unusual semi-darkness where the snow seemed to reflect even the smallest of light from a solitary street lamp, decoration, or passing car into something ethereal. As we passed by each small town, more cars left our long train, and by evening, we were one of few cars left on the road.

I looked over at mom who had both hands tight on the steering wheel.

"I wonder where your father is," she exclaimed with a worried voice. "Surely he is right behind us, but I don't want to stop because we may get stuck out here."

Neither my sister nor I said anything as our car moved slowly toward our destination.

We finally made it across the Tennessee River over to Florence. Our last obstacle was the ride up the long hill from the river to the town. Fortunately, the road had been reasonably cleared with all of the vehicles driving on it all day. We still held our breaths as we made our way up Court Street and turned right onto Tennessee Street, our tires occasionally losing traction momentarily when they hit an icy patch.

Christmas decorations were all over the downtown area as we drove by. Their light reflecting on the snow and ice somehow made the outside seem warmer than it really was. Since it was now past six in the evening, most of the stores and businesses had already closed and the streets were somewhat empty. We were almost there! A few blocks down, we turned left onto Walnut Street, and I saw Sears and Roebuck on the left and my grandmother's house on the right.

Her house sat on a corner lot and was an old, white Victorian of simple character and southern charm. In her parlor, there was a big, bay window looking south toward where we were coming, and as we drove up to her house, I saw my grandmother anxiously looking outside in anticipation of our arrival.

###

December 15

A Southern Snowstorm – Part 2

Grandmother was born in that house shortly after her parents built it. When she married my grandfather, they lived in the house with her parents and also raised three children. My father was actually born in one of the back north-facing bedrooms. My grandfather had passed before I was born, and grandmother lived in the house by herself with the occasional long-term visit from her sister.

Grandmother knew we were coming, and as always, she had the porch lights turned on for us. Because she lived by herself and was getting on in the years, there were not many Christmas decorations around the house. However, the vision of my grandmother in the window made the house a welcomed sight.

Mom pulled into the driveway, and the back door to the house opened. My grandmother poked her head out into the cold weather.

"Clara, I am glad you are here. We have been so worried about you."

She then looked around expecting something else. "Where's Ben?" she asked with surprise.

"We don't know," my mother replied. "We lost him outside of Huntsville, and he never caught up with us."

"Oh my," exclaimed my grandmother. Now grandmother never once used any type of profanity of which I was ever aware. She was also very careful in how she spoke and communicated with others. However, she had a special way of saying "Oh, my." It was part raspy. It was part soft. It was part guttural. It was singularly demonstrative and simplistically to the point. In short, her use of "Oh, my," clearly expressed her sentiments over what vast oratories or bawdy expletives could never do.

We all walked into the house from the back door and entered the enclosed back porch where the earthen and clammy smells from within reminded me of summers long past. We then entered grandmother's warm kitchen where the aromas of a day's worth of cooking and baking enticed my nose. I quickly grabbed onto grandmother and gave her a most substantial hug. She hugged me back, laughed, and helped me off with my coat. We quickly passed through the dining room where the feast would take place the next day, and we made our way toward the parlor where, waiting for us, were other members of my dad's family.

"Oh, look at you two," my Aunt Biddy said joyfully to my sister and me as she bent down with her arms stretched out wide. "You have grown so much. Come here and give your aunt a hug."

That was all the invitation that I needed. I ran to her arms and held her tight. This was the lady with the chocolate pound cake. This was the lady whose laugh and rich southern accent were infectious, and I wanted as much of them as I could get. Soon, I heard a booming voice in the room.

"Put her right there, boy!" my uncle Charlie said as he stretched out his hand in invitation to a grown-up, mainly handshake. As I took his hand, he pretended to act surprised at how a young boy of my size had such a substantial grip. There are many words to describe my uncle Charlie. Warm, funny, strict, opinionated, patriotic, and loving are just some of the adjectives that were squeezed into his six-foot frame and balding head. Later in life, it would be Uncle Charlie who would teach me about strong character and undeniable patriotism. I loved him for those gifts.

Also in the room were my aunt and uncle's three children who were much older than we were. There stood Blair who was a clean-shaven, handsome younger man whose chuckle and big smile came directly from his father. Next was Jeb. He was the oldest with dark, curvy hair and dapper good looks. He always seemed very smart and articulate to me. Nancy, my other cousin, was just simply a pretty young lady. She had dark hair and a warm southern accent much like her mother's. I always liked it when Nancy was around because, while the older people were busy playing cards, talking, or watching various football games, she always took time to play games with me. They were all there in the room, and we felt very welcomed.

Looking around the room, I spotted a couple of candy dishes sitting on bookcases in the parlor. I don't know if it was due to my short size or the fact that I had a built-in radar to detect candy, but no matter where grandmother put the Christmas candy, I could always find it. One dish had soft caramels of various flavors. I would always take a couple of pieces for now and put one or two more in my pocket for later. The other dish usually had hard Christmas candy popping with bright colors. While I had my favorites from this dish, all of it was good. As I slipped a piece of the hard candy into my mouth I heard my aunt talking from the other side of the parlor.

"My, my, Clara. You mean you lost sight of Ben outside of Huntsville?"

Mom then told the family of the horrible driving conditions and how we lost dad who had been behind us for most of the trip, but who eventually got cut off by other cars.

Grandmother then looked at mom with worry. "I hope he is not stuck somewhere and can't get out."

The happiness and joy I had been feeling then quickly changed again to concern over my dad. I didn't know where he was, and I wished I had ridden with him so that I could have been there, even if I didn't really know what I would have done if I were with him.

Soon, I saw my cousins Blair and Jeb buttoning up their coats. "I think we will go out there and try to find him," Blair said as he and his brother Jeb slipped their hands inside their gloves.

They turned to mom with reassuring smiles. "We will follow the route you took, and we should be able to find him soon."

As the door to the parlor opened, the cold, icy weather quickly entered the heated room and everyone shivered. The cold and dark outside only served to increase my concern and anxiety over my dad. He should have been here by now. I really wanted him in our warm parlor talking with all of us and enjoying Christmas.

My mind then turned to what had recently happened with our President and how the country must have felt both loss and hopelessness. At my young age, I had yet to experience real loss. However, I really missed my dad, and my mind was soon filled with all kinds of thoughts – none of them good – and I worried that my cousins would not be able to find him. I guess my mom and cousin Nancy sensed my distress. They came over to me and tried to reassure me. "Drew, don't worry, your cousins will find your father," my mom said as she gave me a reassuring hug. Nancy then bent down to my eye level.

"Hey, Drew, why don't you come upstairs with us to your bedroom, and we'll get you dressed for bed," she said as she put her finger on my nose and twitched it back and forth. "Maybe your dad will be home soon, and you can see him before you go to bed."

As I walked up the long, curved staircase to my room, my thoughts were no longer about Christmas, or Santa, or food. They were focused on my dad and where he could be on this cold and horrible winter's night. While mom and Cousin Nancy helped me unpack my suitcase and get ready for bed,

I worried that my dad would be too cold or that my cousins would miss him because of the snow that could accumulate on his car.

After I changed my clothes, mom and I walked downstairs. She said she would fix my sister and me some cookies and milk before bed. To this day, I don't remember what kind of cookies they were or what they tasted like. I just remember having a huge lump in my throat and that I was concerned about my dad. Afterwards, amid the murmurs and whispers of the adults in the parlor, I walked back upstairs. Mom followed, placing her hand on my shoulder.

Walking into my bedroom, I felt helpless and afraid. However, just when I thought I couldn't take it anymore, I heard footsteps on the front porch outside. The footsteps then changed to the sound of stomping, shuffling feet as those who were outside were trying to remove snow from their shoes. The parlor door abruptly opened to the sounds of cheers and greetings. Mom and I ran down the stairs to see my dad and cousins removing their snow-covered coats and getting well-deserved hugs from grandmother and my aunt.

I ran over and hugged my dad whose coat and body were still cold from the night air. A little of the snow that was on him fell into my pajama collar and down my back, accentuating to me just how cold it was outside.

We all sat around the parlor as dad told us what had happened. It seemed that when he got cut off from us, he was still able to make good time until there was a wreck and he was in stand-still traffic for over an hour until it cleared. He said that all he could think about was getting home to his family. He was just outside Florence when he saw car lights flashing and heard a horn blowing. He realized it was Jeb and Blair, and he knew he would be at grandmother's house soon.

We were all very happy, and the festive atmosphere became more so as we all stayed there in the warm parlor a little longer to catch up on what everybody had been doing during the year. Then mom stood up and said, "Time to go to bed." And my sister and I started walking back up the big, curvy staircase.

All of a sudden, my thoughts turned again to Christmas Eve and whether Santa could find us. After all, we were six hours away from home, and everything was covered in snow. Worse yet, grandmother's house only had coal-burning fireplaces that had been converted to ceramic gas heaters. They were too small for Santa. I was mortified. However, I wanted to make sure I didn't show my concern. Like the rest of us, mom had a long day. She had also told me that morning that Santa knew where we were, and quite frankly, after the night's ordeal, my worry about Santa Clause soon faded to tired satisfaction now that dad was home.

On Christmas morning when I awoke, snow was still on the ground. The day was clear again, and I could hear the wind rustling the trees and rattling the old Victorian house. I walked downstairs and heard grandmother whistling in the kitchen, as she always did when she was making breakfast. I don't know if it was the cold weather, the anticipation of grandmother's great breakfast, or that dad was here safe and sound, but I was just plain hungry. I was looking forward to all of the food that Christmas and my entire family would bring. As I turned the corner past the staircase, I glanced into the parlor to see if mom and dad were there. I was shocked at what I saw. I stood there dumbfounded as I looked over an absolute wonderment of toys and games awaiting my sister and me. Santa came! Mom was right! He knew where we were!

My hunger temporarily left me as I ran over to my presents. That year I got a fire truck, a gray plastic fire ax, and a yellow fire helmet. I looked an absolute sight running around grandmother's house wearing my pajamas, robe, and my new fireman's equipment. I also got a toy garage where I could push my cars into, as well as a toy gas pump that had some type of orange liquid inside that would drain down to the base of the pump as if I were actually putting gas in a car. It was all there: a collection of small airplanes, some new clothes, a few games, and my stocking that was filled to the brim with candy, nuts, and fruit. It was leaning by the bookcase next to the fireplace – the same bookcase where the Christmas candy dish was the night before.

We had a wonderful Christmas that year. As my family traditionally did, we all met at grandmother's house for Christmas dinner. We were now joined by my father's other sister, Mary Elizabeth and my Uncle Bob. There was food everywhere. It was just how I imagined and better! After dinner, we gathered around the parlor to digest the huge portions we had just consumed and maybe watch a little football on grandmother's RCA color "round eye" console.

We then loaded up the cars and drove a few miles over to my aunt's house where she always had a beautiful Christmas tree that was covered underneath with all of the family's presents.

With a fire burning in the fireplace, Christmas music coming softly from a stereo in a nearby room, and all of us opening presents and sharing our stories, I couldn't help but think that the trauma of the night before made this Christmas seem closer and better to me.

Later that evening, after all of the wrapping paper was cleared, and another log placed on the fire, mom would usually read the Christmas story from St. Luke. From that year on, whenever she read that story, I always worried that the Baby Jesus was not warm enough in the cold night. I was reassured when I would look at a nativity scene and saw the animals so close by. I knew they would keep Him warm.

As the fire popped and crackled in the living room, I lay on the floor by myself looking at the tree. I could hear most of my family in the den cheering on their favorite football team, as well as my mom, grandmother, and aunt in the kitchen washing dishes. I thought briefly about our country's loss and how horrible that must have been. I also thought of how many more families this year were sharing the season and comforting each other much like mom and my Cousin Nancy reassured and comforted me with their warm hugs.

It occurred to me that when families get together during times of either sadness or joy, something good usually comes out of it. I also began to learn something important about Christmas. As a little boy was able to in his small mind, I began to realize that the magic of Christmas might not be defined as much from presents, food, or Santa. The real magic of Christmas comes from understanding the warmth, love, and promise of

Jesus, as well as the celebration of the season's warmth with family, no matter where we were.

It was a bitterly cold and snowy Christmas in 1963, but it warmed my heart greatly.

###

December 16

The Christmas Ornament

I am sure everyone who decorates for Christmas has a favorite adornment or trimming that, without it, the season would not seem complete. In fact, there are some who are almost ritualistic in the type of decorations they use and where they should be placed.

For instance, some like bubble lights, while some have a special figurine or stuffed animal they like. Others have a special Christmas candle of which they are especially fond or maybe a decoration that has been passed down from generation to generation. Still others like to use decorations to rekindle simpler, homespun times. To these people live, fragrant evergreens must always adorn a house.

In short, if I were to mention the word Christmas, I bet there would be one decoration that would come to mind which would reawaken special memories or serve as a consistent comfort to an ever-changing, fast-paced world. My favorite decoration happens to be an old, solitary, glass ornament of no great significance or notoriety. It is known in our family as "Drew's ornament."

This favorite ornament of mine was made over fifty years ago by the Shiny Brite Company in New York City. During this time, there were a few American companies that did a good job capturing the quality and craftsmanship of the much older and more established German ornament makers. The ornament is about five inches around with an opaque fuchsia base adorned with a white snow scene relief. The scene is similar to what one would find on a Currier and Ives Christmas card, yet simpler.

I don't know why I liked that ornament so much. I mean, there were many other ornaments on our family tree that were larger, had more color, or were more elaborate in their decoration. But this one ornament seemed to call out to me when I was a little boy and has been my favorite ever since. It didn't take long for mom to realize that this Christmas ball was my favorite as she would always hang it on the lower right side of the tree closer to my eye level. Even as I grew older and taller, my favorite ornament always hung in the same place, as if the tree were never taken down after each Christmas.

Without fail, whenever I sat in my parent's living room to look at the tree, my eye would always work its way down the brightly colored branches to that one little Christmas ball.

As I looked at the ornament, I saw a sleigh plowing through a snowy wood on its way to the little town nearby. The stars hung high in the night sky. One star was particularly large and reminded me of the Christmas star. Although the scene on the ornament was probably from the late 1800's, it was always comforting to me to know that the Star of Bethlehem is always with us.

As a boy, sometimes, I would sit on the floor beside the tree. While my sister was always looking at the name tags of the gifts under the tree, I would gaze at the tree itself and look closely at "my" ball. I always wondered who the people in the sleigh were going to see. Did they have Christmas dinner tucked away snuggly under the buffalo robes protecting the riders? Were they going to church for a midnight Christmas Eve celebration? Were they coming home after a visit with friends or relatives who lived out in the country?

I could almost hear the runners hiss through the dense snow pack as the muffled hooves of the horses galloped closer to the town. I could imagine a smart crack of the whip as the driver anticipated warmer quarters ahead, while the rhythmic breathing and grunting of the horses mingled with the glistening silver harness bells as they broke the silence of the cold, crisp evening air.

Maybe it was the color of the ornament that caught my eye. The reddish-pink color seemed to capture the full essence of colored lights on the tree, and its shade reminded me of the look and taste of my favorite hard Christmas candy. In short, I believe that one ornament encompasses most of what this time of year means to me.

As time passed, my parents became too old to put up the tree, and most of their Christmas decorations were tucked away in the basement. A few years ago, my mom gave me the ornament for my family's tree. Now, whenever I look at the large Christmas tree in our den, my eyes work their way down the branches of multi-colored lights to the lower right side where an old, glass ornament of special importance is hung bravely on a limb for me to enjoy and recapture some pleasant memories.

###

December 17

Christmas Custard

To me, there are only a few of the seasonal pleasantries in life that inextricably define themselves as to what Christmas is or what Christmas ought to be. Boiled custard is one of them. Dipping a ladle into a bowl of the frothy goodness, I eagerly await its sweet and savory flavors. The palatable aroma and taste of boiled custard gently awakens the sights, sounds, and smells of Christmases past, and I savor each with every sip.

Now, down in the South, we call this heavenly concoction boiled custard. Elsewhere it is called *crème anglaise,* which is French for English cream. While custard is considered to be a French delicacy, it is believed that the ancient Romans used variations of it for sauces and creams. In the Middle Ages, custards were used with all kinds of foods including meats, fish, fruits, and pastries.

Our Southern holiday favorite is made into a drink and has the simple ingredients of eggs, milk, cream, vanilla, and sugar. It is prepared using a double boiler, a lot of patience, and is usually served either hot or cold. Some top it with meringue and garnish with cinnamon or chocolate shavings. Some even add alcohol to it. I prefer mine plain.

It should be clearly noted that boiled custard is not egg nog. Some say that boiled custard is a southern treat, while egg nog is its Yankee cousin. Boiled custard requires all of the ingredients to be cooked while traditional egg nog is not. Furthermore, eggnog usually has nutmeg and other spices while boiled custard does not. While I like both, boiled custard is my favorite.

After Christmas dinner up in Florence, Alabama, the whole family consisting of grandmother, mom, dad, sister, aunts, uncles, and various assorted cousins and kin would gather into the living room to "have the tree," which was our ritual of exchanging gifts. At some point toward the end of it, grandmother would walk through the living room toward the kitchen.

When all of the paper, ribbons, boxes, and bows had been cleared away, along came grandmother with her boiled custard in a glass bowl on a silver tray with red glass cups surrounding it. She would proudly set it on the already cleared dining room table. Following behind her would be my aunt with her homemade chocolate pound cake, which was the perfect companion to the golden liquid mixture awaiting us.

Everyone would gather around the punchbowl and cake, with cup in hand and mouths watering in anticipation. The ladle would dip the custard from the bowl and transfer the frothy goodness to our ruby-red glasses. Now, while I couldn't prove that those hundred year-old faceted glasses made the custard taste better, they sure did add to the experience.

The deep, rich red of the glass contrasted nicely with the custard inside, and the thick glass and gentle curve at the base made this a substantial container for the celebratory drink of Christmas. While the glasses were like large gems themselves, they gave added pleasure when they mirrored the warm glow of the candles or reflected the multi-colored lights from the Christmas tree.

After everyone's cup had been filled, we would all raise them up and wish each other "Merry Christmas!" and I would quickly find a place to sit down and enjoy my treat. The cool liquid felt good going down, and the taste lingered on my taste buds in preparation for a forkful of the chocolate pound cake. At that point, I didn't care about any of my gifts. The boiled custard took my full, undivided attention.

The custard was so thick that it would coat the red glass. I would turn the cup upside down to drain as much of its goodness as I could. When the entire family was present, there was usually only enough custard for one serving each. There were a few years when not everybody could make it for the holidays. During those years, I was allowed to get a little extra from the bowl.

The only time I drink boiled custard is during the Christmas holidays. With today's modern conveniences though, one can actually buy boiled custard at the store rather than take the time to make it. However, the homemade version is always better. No matter how I get it, though, from the first taste until the last drop, boiled custard takes me back to the warmth and comfort of Christmases past.

###

December 18

Christmas Without Dad

In September of 2011, my Dad passed away. It happened suddenly, and although he probably felt little pain, it really shocked me and my family greatly. I got through the funeral and most of the weeks afterwards by trying to take care of Mom who, obviously, was having a difficult time with the reality of it all. During the occasional times I would visit the house, there were so many things around that reminded me of him. Other than my grandmother who was the only living grandparent when I was born, my father was the only close relative of mine to pass away. It was devastating, to say the least.

As the months crawled by, I remember being in my den one night, sipping my tea and looking at our Christmas tree. It suddenly hit me that this would be the first Christmas without my Dad. As I looked up and down that tree, I remembered the times when I was a boy that he and I would help Mom get the decorations down from the attic. Now, Dad was not a do-it-yourself kind of guy, so after the boxes of decorations were stacked in the den and living room, Dad would read his book or watch a football game. As the boxes were emptied, he would carefully place them back in the attic.

Looking at the colored lights on my tree, I remembered the times when Dad would complain about people who didn't use colored lights in their decorations. "All of these white lights...I just don't understand it," he would say. "Colored lights are much cheerier and Christmassy than those white lights." As it turned out, he didn't much care for the new colored LED lights either. He said they looked too artificial.

My Christmas memories with my Dad are plentiful. I remember cuddling up to him in his big easy chair while he would read Christmas stories to me. I would be in my flannel pajamas, and he and I would have cups of hot chocolate and some of Mom's seven layer cookies in hand. Dad always loved food. He was the one who taught me how to cook a turkey to where the meat would just about fall off the bone. He also taught me how to carve the turkey and strip all of the meat from the bones.

Dad was also the king of the turkey sandwich. Now, most families get tired of turkey after a day or so of holiday eating. Not my family. In fact, Dad would always buy the largest turkey he could so that we would have plenty of leftovers. On December 26th, we could count on two things. First, our neighbor across the street would toss out her tree to the side of the road for trash pick-up. Second, my Dad would be in the kitchen making turkey sandwiches.

During the holidays, dad loved to play board games. When I was little, he always made sure that he would play games that I liked, and if I was having a difficult time, he would see to it that I would win one or two games. Dad loved games that tested one's memory and intellect. Dad taught me how to play cards. Specifically, he taught me how to play poker. During the holidays when I was in high school, my friends would love to come over to the house and play poker with me and my Dad. While my Dad was a competitor, to him, winning or losing never seemed as important as setting aside the time to play with friends and family. That is what made him really happy.

I remember when I got my first bike. It had training wheels on it. As a young boy, I was a little afraid of falling, so I never really wanted him to take off those wheels. I remember that, after much coaching and encouragement from him, I allowed Dad to remove them. He assured me he would be right by my side as I rode my bike. For the first few minutes he was…then I noticed I was riding all by myself. My solo experience on the bicycle was a thrill that both he and I enjoyed over his favorite drink, an ice cold Dr. Pepper.

Dad was the one who operated the movie camera as I hung up my stocking for Santa on Christmas Eve and the next morning as I inspected what Santa left for me. He was the one who unpacked all of the pieces to my Major Matt Mason Space Station and helped me to build it. He was the one who taught me to love and appreciate all of the old Christmas movies, and he was the one who gave my wife-to-be a big hug of acceptance as we announced around the tree on Christmas Day in 1982 that we were going to be married.

I remember one year when we got a table tennis table for Christmas. Now, table tennis was something that my Dad loved to play. In fact, when he was in the Air Force, he won trophies for playing the game. I remember his teaching me how to hold the "bat" and how to play strategically. After a while, I could actually beat him in a few games. He and I would play for hours and hours down in our basement until mom would call us up for dinner.

My Dad always encouraged me. He would always listen with delight as I told him about some exploit I had done or honor I had won. When I brought home bad grades during a tough semester, he would encourage me to buckle down and do better. One year when I was in third grade, our teacher sent us home for the Christmas holidays with an assignment to hand write every word in the *Declaration of Independence*. While Dad couldn't do the writing for me, I remember how he helped me by bringing hot chocolate and some of Mom's cookies to the breakfast table where I was working.

Dad taught me how to throw a football and how to shoot a bb gun. One Christmas when we were at grandmother's house, Dad gave me his old toy army soldiers and showed me how he used to set them up and keep count of the casualties or how much his army had advanced.

Dad also taught me how to build a fire in the fireplace. He and I became the official builders of the fire and keepers of the flame in our house. When the fire would start to die out, he and I would go outside and pick choice pieces of wood from those that were stacked up by the side of the house. Then he would show me how to gently place the logs on the fire to ensure maximum heat.

When my twins were born, Dad started to teach them many of the things that he taught me. When the twins would open their gifts at Christmastime, Dad would show his excitement as they ran around the room with their new toys he got them. Dad also like to read to them much as he read to me. In fact, my Dad taught me the overall love and enjoyment of books.

As I sipped the last of my tea while looking at the tree in my den before going to bed, I knew that I missed my Dad, and Christmas would not be the same without him. However, I also realized that much of what Dad liked and taught me still lives within me and within my children. While I miss him, I cherish all of the wonderful memories he gave me. The most important thing Dad taught me, however, was how to be a good Dad. Every day I honor him by trying to be the best Dad I can be to my two children. During Christmas dinner as I carve the turkey and watch all of its juiciness gush forth to the cheers of my twins, I close my eyes for a brief instant, look up to the sky, and thank my Dad.

###

December 19

Exchanging Gifts

Now that I've grown older, the idea of exchanging Christmas gifts with friends and family has lost some of its appeal. Clearly, the tradition of giving someone a gift during this time of the year harkens back to that special night when the three wise men brought gifts of gold, frankincense, and myrrh to the Christ Child in the manger. This gesture of the wise men was appropriate considering who the Baby was. However, it is also poignant that, years afterwards, those two precious spices were also used on Christ's lifeless body after he was removed from the cross and sealed in the tomb.

In contrast, today's gift giving oftentimes has little thought to it and usually winds up being a cold, meaningless gift card or some last-minute gadget bought on sale at one of the many retailers who have succeeded in commercializing the season to the point of being beyond recognition.

There was a point in my lifetime, however, where gift giving was fun and meaningful and the gifts themselves were more thoughtful than extravagant. I remember when I was a child, we would oftentimes travel up to Florence, Alabama, to spend Christmas with my grandmother and other relatives. A couple of months beforehand, my mom and dad would spend time thinking of each family member and making decisions on what to get them. Shortly after Thanksgiving, my mom would usually start wrapping the gifts and labeling them so that my grandmother would not get the shotgun shells meant for my uncle or one of my cousins would not get the bathrobe meant for my aunt.

As she wrapped each gift, she would carefully place it under our tree. By the time Christmas came, the area underneath the tree would be filled to capacity. Back then each gift was hand wrapped – gift bags were either not around or were unheard of for such an occasion. I remember when I would go into the living room during the evening to look at the tree, I loved admiring all of the nicely wrapped gifts with their assorted styles of wrapping paper.

One year, mom bought a fairly large roll of wrapping paper that I especially liked. It didn't have fat Santas, scrumptious candy canes, flying reindeer, or joyful cartoon figures on it. Nor did it have green holly, silver bells, sparkling ornaments, or red poinsettias on it. We referred to it as the pine cone paper. It was simple and had brown pine cones on a green background with snow gently covering the scales and prickles of each cone. There was the occasional red berry to add a little color to it, but it didn't "scream" Christmas like the other wrapping paper did. It was natural and peaceful.

Unlike today's thin and flimsy paper, the wrapping paper of my childhood was very thick and sturdy. When people would unwrap their gifts, they would try to save as much of the paper to reuse for the next year. After the second or third year, it was apparent that the pine cone paper was going to stick around for a while. In fact, it got to where it wouldn't be Christmas without at least one gift wrapped in the recycled conifer covering. If my recollection serves me correctly, I believe we got 12 years of usage out of that paper until we just couldn't find a piece large enough to use. I wish I still had a piece of that pine cone paper.

Anyway, after a large dinner at my grandmother's house, we would all load up in various vehicles for the short drive to my aunt's house. There, we would all pile into her living room where there was a large Christmas tree with gifts around it. All the rest of the family brought our gifts from our cars to place around the tree. Soon, it looked as though the entire living room was filled with every shape and size of gift imaginable. We would then begin the ritual of, what my family called, "Having the Tree." For about three hours, we would all sit around the tree while Uncle Charlie or one of my cousins would pick up an individual gift and read out loud what was on the card. Sometimes it was just a plain card like "To Grandmother, From The Lunas." Other times, the card had a little endearing humor to it, like "To the Best Wife I've Ever Had, From Ben." Now, my mom was dad's only wife, but everyone in the room got the humor in the card and laughed accordingly.

Each person received a gift one at a time. Each person unwrapped his or her gift and held it up for all to see. Sometimes there were gasps of amazement and awe. Other times, there was laughter and hand clapping. No one was ever skipped. I was often amazed at how Uncle Charlie could pick out gifts from the somewhat haphazardly arranged pile to make sure that everyone had a turn opening a gift until all of the gifts had been opened.

Afterwards, we would all gather up the bows to save for future Christmases and scout around for wrapping paper that could be folded up and recycled. The paper that could not be reused was carefully put in the fireplace where we could all watch the various inks on the paper ignite and turn the flames into multiple festive colors. Our attention then focused on the dining room table where there was grandmother's boiled custard and my aunt's chocolate pound cake.

Now, isn't it funny that when you grow up with these types of traditions, you automatically assume that all families do the same thing? I mean, who would think of celebrating Christmas without having the tree followed by boiled custard and cake afterward? Well, I married my wife and entered into a wonderful but completely different world of her family with their own set of traditions.

While my mom and dad were mainly raised in and around the town of Florence, my in-laws are more country folk who were raised deep in the northern countryside of Tuscaloosa County. Most of the food on their Christmas table was grown or hunted on their land. While my mother-in-law was a staunch Baptist lady who would never allow drinking in her house, she always had a small bottle of whiskey secretly hidden up on the top shelf that was used to make her friendship cake that, quite frankly, had the great tastes of all of the holidays of the year rolled into one fantastic treat.

After dinner, the Lynn family would gather around the den. I sat down on the couch, watching a little football while a small, three-foot tree shined brightly next to it. I fully expected that someone from the family would start to call out names on the packages and hand them out one by one. Not there. The children in the family rushed over to where the gifts were and started ripping open gifts, throwing paper and ribbons in the air. A few family members would pass out the rest of the gifts, and everyone opened his or his at the same time. Again, however, there were sometimes gasps of amazement and awe while other times, there was laughter and hand clapping. Afterward, we had to dig through the mounds of paper and ribbon to make sure a child had not been buried alive.

With both families, however, the gifts given were usually not extravagant or costly. However, a lot of thought was put into them, and they were all given from the heart. I always felt like I came out on the winning end because, in addition to the boiled custard and chocolate pound cake of my family, I also got to enjoy my mother-in-law's friendship cake, tea cake cookies, and plenty of her hot coffee. Traditions are fun and enjoyable. However, enjoying new experiences with the best in-laws I could ever ask for has been a new-found treasure for me.

No matter how your family spends Christmas together, as long as it is with love and thoughtfulness, you are living in the true spirit of the season. Now, to make this Christmas truly special, forget the gift cards and gadgets and get or make something truly special for your friends and family. In your special gift, they will not only unwrap the joy with which you gave it to them, they will also unwrap memories that will be shared for many Christmases to come.

###

December 20

Christmas Lights

It was a tradition of my family that, on some evening during the holidays, we would all bundle up, get into our car, and drive around the town to look at Christmas decorations. I always looked forward to this night because the air was usually cold, the variety of lights was to fun to see, and afterwards, we would always convene back in our den for hot chocolate and popcorn while watching a favorite Christmas movie.

We would start the night driving around our neighborhood looking at the decorations of our friends and neighbors. We would pass by the house on the corner that always had the same beautiful decorations year after year. Soon, we passed by the house that had the big blue lighted star perched high on the rooftop. Driving around to the school, we saw the house with the lighted manger and the house with the life-sized Santa Claus winking at us.

Some of the houses had sparse decorations consisting of a wreath on a spot-lighted door with electric candles in the windows. Others had lights outlining the house, wrapped around the bushes, and hanging from the gutters. It was always amazing to me at how many different ways people could decorate for Christmas. Just when I thought I had seen it all, along would come another unique house.

Then we would drive to the downtown area where we were met with lighted Santa Claus faces, giant candy canes, and trumpeted angles hanging from the streetlights welcoming onlookers and proclaiming the arrival of the joyous season. Storefronts along the streets outlined their windows with multi-colored lights, displayed Christmas trees, and hung garland around their buildings and doorways. A few stores went "old school" and frosted their windows and decorated in a Victorian theme. I half expected Ebenezer Scrooge to come out of one of these stores with the Ghost of Christmas Past following closely behind.

There were two years when I was in college that, for one reason or another, Tuscaloosa did not decorate its city streets for Christmas. It was a horrible time. I mean, even small towns nearby with only one or two traffic lights managed to dress their streets up for the holidays. Tuscaloosa was a large university town that should have known better than to not decorate. I was a student journalist at the time, and I decided to write a story about the travesty. The story was picked up by *USA Today,* and afterwards, my phone rang off the wall with people cheering me on as well as some not-so-happy city leaders. However, from that point forward, Tuscaloosa has never skipped a year decorating for Christmas.

After driving through the city, we usually stopped by a couple of the poorer sections of the area. Here, we would often see a spectacle of lights. Some houses had thousands and thousands of multi-colored lights complete with mangers, life-sized figurines, and various greetings spelled out in lights. On most nights these neighborhoods had long lines of cars waiting to see the displays. As a child, it amazed me to look at the joy and happiness displayed upon homes whose owners had very little to be thankful for in the material sense. However, they seemed to understand the real meaning of the light and hope of the season.

We would drive out into the country where the blackness of night would soon be interrupted by a splash of Christmas lights from solitary farmhouses scattered throughout the land. Passing by a pasture of cows grazing on the frosty grass nearby, I would roll down my window for a brief instant to smell the earthiness and richness of the rural night air. I caught a whiff of the cows nearby and thought to myself that these were the first aromas the Christ Child smelled as he lay in a feeding crib among the livestock in the manger. I looked up at the bright, clear stars in the sky as our car meandered its way through the dark, quiet road while "Away in a Manger" played on the radio.

Our trip would not be complete without stopping by some of the more affluent neighborhoods. The size and splendor of the houses always amazed me, and as a young boy, I had fancies of being in one of those houses, sitting in a leather chair by the fire sipping my tea. My fantasy was soon interrupted by my dad exclaiming, "Look at all of these white lights. Don't they believe in pretty colored lights?" Then dad would turn onto the next block and would spot a house he liked saying, "See, the colored lights look so much more cheery that just those plain, old white lights."

As we headed back home, the hum of the car engine and the sounds of Christmas songs on the radio made me feel warm, relaxed, and comfortable. We would soon round the corner to the block where our house was located. We would all marvel at the decorations around our house, and my dad would always complement my mom on the wonderful job she did with decorating.

As we pulled into the carport, I could almost taste the hot chocolate that would soon be ready for us. Every year we did this same routine, and every year I looked forward to it and enjoyed it. While the individual years are now blurred, the bright Christmas decorations we saw have been forever burned into my memory, and I look forward when I extend the tradition with my own family each year.

###

December 21

Sparse Decorations

I accepted a new job in Georgia during the summer of 1999. However, it took us a little while to find a buyer for our house in Louisville, Kentucky. We finally got a contract during the first part of December with closing occurring in January. There was a lot of work to do before we could move. It was not easy packing up a house when I was living almost 500 miles away and my wife was taking care of our two-year-old twins. During the time I had taken off, we quickly wrapped and packed everything that wasn't essential to our short time remaining in the house. The bitter truth to this story was that we were faced with the reality that there would be no decorations for Christmas that year.

Now, I know that Christmas should mean more than green trees, sparkling tinsel, and bright colored lights. I'm fully aware that the true meaning of Christmas should be internal rather than external. After all, how did our soldiers endure the discomfort and loneliness of the many Christmases away from family and hearthside? The thought of our not being able to decorate for Christmas paled in comparison. However, I did feel a little sad.

While I tend to be utilitarian, I just had to openly celebrate in some small way. In my head, I argued that decorations were more for my twins. In reality, I wanted them also. I went to the basement to gaze at all of the boxes we had packed and secured. In the far back I saw a small box about two feet tall and half a foot wide. It was the small Christmas tree I used for my office at work. It would be perfect because it was easy to set up and take down after the holidays.

I quickly hurried up the stairs, opened the box, and pulled out the tree. Clearly, it was not as grand as our much larger tree. However, it did have a pretty simplicity to it that rekindled a vague recollection of my parents' small tree at the Air Force base where my father was stationed when I was about two. The tree also reminded me that we should be counting all of our blessings no matter how large or small. After all, we had finally sold our house and were about to be a family again. To me, that was the best present of all.

I looked around our den to find a decent place to put the tree. I wanted it on a table where the twins could look at it closely. I chose the end table that sat between our two recliners. That way, I could keep an eye on the tree in case they decided to play with it. I sat the tree on the table and plugged it into the wall. Although sparse, it looked pretty and welcoming. Now Santa would have a proper location to drop off his presents.

As the days to Christmas shortened, my wife and I were still busy packing. We did, however, manage to watch some Christmas cartoons and eat some homemade cookies with our twins. During the evening hours, I would turn off all of the lights in the den except for the tree. Its glow filled the room with warmth and happiness. At that point it seemed that our little tree bravely put out the light of trees much larger and more ornate. On Christmas Eve, we all gathered around the tree while I pulled out a picture book of "Twas the Night Before Christmas." After the story, we put the twins to bed, and my wife and I spent a little quiet time relaxing.

Between the packing, taking care of the twins, and celebrating Christmas a little, we failed to watch any of the local news and weather. All that day we had been playing Christmas music, watching movies, or playing with the twins. What we didn't know was that a big cold front was moving down from Chicago. I could feel it getting colder when I went outside occasionally, but I had no idea what was in store the next day. Tired and worn out from packing, we went upstairs to bed, leaving the lights on our little tree burning brightly.

When I woke up the next morning, I was amazed to see almost a foot of snow on the lawn. I was thrilled because the last white Christmas I remembered was when I was four years old. I quickly woke up my wife to wish her a "Merry White Christmas," and I hurried down to the kitchen to make coffee. Our den had a large sliding glass door, and opening the blinds, I could see the snow was packed right up to the edge of the house. Through all of this whiteness, our little tree shined bravely and brightly. Then, the reality of everything hit me.

While I enjoyed our little tree, I missed our larger tree, the mantle decorations, and our Christmas village. Looking outside, however, I realized that God gave us the best decorations ever. It was a live Christmas village complete with real snow! It was a natural beauty that could not be imitated by man-made objects. Looking out on the lawn, I noticed the snow covered our green holly trees that were teaming with large, red berries sparkling in the sunlight. As the children came down to open their presents, I marveled at the joy and beauty of it all. That year, God helped us decorate for Christmas and used our sparse little tree to make me appreciate the abundance we had.

###

December 22

Christmas Goodies

I have a simple warning for anyone who reads *A Christmas Carol* by Charles Dickens. Make sure you have eaten first. For Dickens has a way of describing every morsel of food – from the ripe pears in the shopkeeper's window to the lovingly prepared Christmas pudding at Bob Crachit's place - so that the reader may extract the maximum taste and pleasure possible from the imagination, only to desire further satisfaction by raiding the cupboard or refrigerator at a later time. Even after a full meal, when sitting down to read Dickens' Christmas story, I require a little hot tea and cookies just in case one of his cleverly turned phrases about a dinner or a confection reawakens my appetite.

It is no secret that food is everywhere at Christmas time. From hams and turkeys to pies and cakes (and everything in between), we are inundated by delicious food during the holidays. Furthermore, everywhere we look, from morning television shows to magazine articles, there are recipes for new dishes we might want to create as well as slight variations to our standby, traditional fare.

Take the turkey for example. My father's tradition was to buy the largest one possible, wake up before sunrise, baste the bird, and cook it "low and slow." By the time 1 p.m. rolled around, the meat was juicy and falling off the bone. However, some people marinate it in a brine or inject it with flavor by using something that looks terrifyingly close to a hypodermic needle. Still others like to deep fry their birds. Now, throwing ole Tom into a vat of hot oil seems somewhat of a sacrilege to me, not to mention the fact that this new tradition has caused a lot of house fires.

Some people like ham for their Christmas dinner. I don't mean just a regular baked ham. I'm talking about one that is slathered in a honey and mustard glaze with whole cloves stuck into the outside of the meat in such a uniform fashion as to resemble soldiers lining up for inspection. On top of all of this covering, some will sweeten it even more with slices of pineapple, oranges, and/or cherries. I usually don't like my meats that sweet. It's Christmas, though, so what the heck?

How about the casseroles? Oh, the casseroles! I'm convinced that women all over the country have formed a secret society complete with confidential handshakes and clandestine symbols to invent new casseroles. They meet every so often to concoct different ways of dumping all sorts of stuff into a pan and baking it at 350 degrees...or until golden brown. With names like Shipwreck, Chicken Old Ladies on a Bus, Slumgullion, and Garbage, one's appetite may fail while wondering what on God's Earth is actually in these dishes. Now, I have dipped a spoon into a few casseroles myself. Some I liked, and some I tried hiding under a piece of lettuce on my plate. However, the holidays bring on a huge casserole parade and one better not be weak at heart or in stomach while engaging in the festivities.

To me, baked goods at Christmas are synonymous with pure joy and contentment. The aroma of hot rolls or cookies from the oven; the pillow-like softness of cakes on the sideboard cooling; and the tastes of vanilla, cinnamon, sugar, nuts, and chocolate all harken us back to simple, pleasant times spent in the kitchens of our mothers or grandmothers as we await what's in store over an ice-cold glass of milk. Cookies are a major part of this holiday staple. I love them hard or soft, hot or cold, decorated or not. My biggest weakness is the Danish butter cookies sold in decorative tins in just about every store during the holidays. Give me some butter cookies and hot tea, and I would reveal government secrets...if I knew any. One year, I was given a four-pound tin of butter cookies. That year, I enjoyed Christmas all the way through to Valentine's Day.

Then, there is chocolate. I can't remember a Christmas when chocolate was not in it. I remember chocolate Santas, chocolate pastries, chocolate cakes, chocolate nougats, and hot chocolate. I believe one of the best Christmas treats ever is the Chocolate Orange. First, it is a fun candy because it comes in a ball wrapped up in orange foil. Before removing the foil, you have to tap it on a flat service to break it into its separate pieces. Opening it reveals little chocolate wedges that look like sections of an orange. Putting one of these wedges in your mouth causes the taste buds to erupt with the warm flavor of the chocolate and the citrusy, tangy flavor of an orange. They are two wonderful combinations.

Aside from all of the fatty Christmas foods out there, the holidays usually bring their share of fruit and nuts to the table. Each year we would have plenty of oranges, apples, and tangerines in our stockings, which also contained an assortment of nuts including Brazil, pecans, walnuts, and almonds. Oftentimes, I remember as a kid, eating the nuts was a great counterbalance to those times when I had eaten just one too many pieces of Christmas candy or chocolate.

In *A Christmas Carol*, the Ghost of Christmas Present carried a horn that he used to sprinkle a magic-like dust over the meals of holiday merrymakers. He told Scrooge that it was his way of making the dinners taste a little more special. There must be something to that because just about everything served at Christmas seems to taste better than during any other time of the year. The mashed potatoes are creamer, the fruit is riper, the turkey is more juicy, the casseroles are more palatable, and the cookies are sweeter.

It may be that our minds have been tricked into thinking that everything should taste better during Christmas. It may be that, due to the love of the season as well as the love we have of our families, more effort is put into cooking during this time of year. However, whether it be through magic dust or thoughtful preparation, the food at this time of year satisfies all of the senses and will forever lock into our Christmas memories.

When I think of Christmas, I think of mom's seven layer cookies, my aunt's chocolate pound cake, and my mother-in-law's hand dipped coconut chocolate candies. To me, it's not Christmas without the aroma of sage and onions of cornbread dressing or the roasted goodness of a turkey in the oven. We would not be truly celebrating the holidays without the dishes of pleasant-tasting hard Christmas candy or chocolate Kisses foil-wrapped in seasonal colors. Santa Claus, in fact, would not be his jolly old self without his treat of cookies and milk by the stockings. I knew one family that insisted Santa would prefer carrots and alfalfa sprouts to sweets. Upon hearing that, I secretly hoped Santa would leave them a lump of coal in their stockings.

I guess the downside to all of this food is all of the weight we gain during our celebrations. Don't listen to the fitness experts, however. There is absolutely no decent low-fat alternative to traditional boiled custard. Christmas comes but once a year, so enjoy all that the season brings…no matter how fattening it is. Right now, I'm going to rustle up some hot tea, pile on a plate full of butter cookies, and enjoy Dickens writing about Christmas food.

###

December 23

Christmas Shopping

I tend not to be a procrastinator when it comes to Christmas shopping. By the time the season winds down to its last few days, I usually have all of my major gifts purchased, wrapped, and stored under the tree. However, many people do wait until the last minute and frantically try to make their way through the throngs of other late shoppers in their quest for gifts.

While I am usually not one of these hurried shoppers, I oftentimes like to be out among them. I enjoy watching the hustle and bustle as they move like cattle through the shopping malls, stopping occasionally to graze at the food court or to find a place of rest among their boxes, bags, and bundles.

A day or two before Christmas, I usually take my children shopping with me. Our list is not big: just some stocking stuffers and goodies. Our main purpose of going is just simply to observe the spectacle of the last-minute shopping of the season.

Walking through the crowds, I see every shape, variety, size, and demeanor of people. Most are what I have come to call "quickly cordial." They are in a hurry to find and purchase their gifts, but not so much so as to refrain from bidding their fellow shoppers a good day, to stop for a moment to exchange pleasantries with someone they know, to help someone pick up their spilled purchases, or to just quickly wish "Merry Christmas" to their fellow shoppers.

As I walk down the mall, I notice the sounds first. I hear two jovial middle-aged men heartily laughing at each other as they leave the card shop. I hear a toddler in her stroller rattling off the list of everything she wants as her mother quickly pushes her past the toy store. I hear the Christmas music out in the mall area as it is awkwardly mixed and mingled with other Christmas songs coming from individual stores.

I catch the conversations of two teen girls walking beside me. I learn from them that Will has been going with Megan for almost three weeks now only to be found hanging out with that sophomore cheerleader with the gap in her teeth; that something called clam diggers are back in style and would make a great Christmas gift; and that Mrs. Johnson is the hardest teacher "in like the whole world." I also hear the rhythmic sound of a small bell as a Salvation Army worker stands by his red kettle thanking shoppers for their generous donations,

while an excited young boy pulls at his father's coat and loud-
ly exclaims that he has found Santa.

Along with the sounds, there are the sights. I turn my head to
see a dapper gentleman wearing a gray buttoned wool sweat-
er and black ivy cap bend over to offer his grandson some of
his cinnamon bun. Down the way is a young couple holding
dearly onto each other as they gaze at the rings in the jewelry
store, and next to them is an elderly couple holding hands
and walking slowly down the mall while the rest of the world
hurries all around them. Decorations and colored lights are
everywhere while shoppers are adorned in their most out-
landish Christmas sweaters and red Santa hats.

Soon, I am overcome by the smells. There is rich, aromatic
coffee mixed with cinnamon near the food court. As I pass the
candle store, I am hit with hundreds of scents all merged into
one. Walking by the tobacconist, I savor the earthy, pungent
aromas of vanilla, bourbon, Latakia, and Cavendish. Greeting
me by one of the larger department stores is a pretty young
lady with samples of sweet and intoxicating perfumes. Next
to her wafts the clean smells of soaps and lotions from the
bath shop next door.

I then walk by the Sears store. I quickly remember when I was
a boy, anxiously awaiting their Christmas catalog in the mail.
I would spend hours looking at all of the toys and deciding
which ones to put on my list. There were very few malls to go
to back then. I also remember the wonderful smells of Sears.
You see, back then, Sears was the only department store I knew
of that also sold chocolates, roasted nuts, and candies by the
pound right in the middle of their store. It was a pleasure just

to walk inside and breathe. I often wonder if the company would not significantly rebound its business if it would just offer those treats again.

Soon, my children find me, and our purchases have been made. We walk through the crowds with smiles on our faces, bidding others "Merry Christmas" as we find our car and head toward the quiet solitude of home. Our little shopping trip became a fun and festive day.

###

December 24

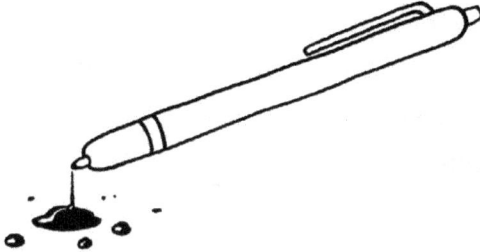

The Church Service

Years ago before our twins were born, my wife and I attended a late-night Christmas Eve service with my parents at their church in Northport, Alabama. As we walked inside, everything was festive and inviting. Green garland with red bows hung throughout the sanctuary, and lighted candles surrounded by holly burned brightly in the sills of the enormous stained glass windows. A large Christmon Tree (Christmons are symbols of the life of Christ) took prominence on the right side of the prayer rail, and the lighted Advent Wreath was centered on the altar.

We were greeted by a variety of cheery folk all dressed in bright Christmas sweaters or wearing festive holiday ties. Children were running around on the thick red-carpeted floor of the church in anticipation of a visit from Santa in a few hours. Soon, the large pipe organ played a Christmas carol, and all of the people settled in the dark oaken pews for the service. All of our family sat in a middle pew toward the middle of the church.

There were greetings and announcements from the minister who was dressed in a beautiful, thick, white robe with a large white satin stole trimmed in gold. The choir then stood to sing the Call to Worship, and the pastor led the congregation in responsive reading and prayer. The next event in the order of worship was the offering. The ushers walked to the front of the church and were handed the heavy brass plates. A prayer was said over them, and then they were soon passed around through the congregation.

While this formality was being done, an elderly plump tenor stood beside the organ to perform his *acapella* rendition of "Sweet Little Jesus Boy." Although his style of singing was better suited for Pavarotti, everyone settled in to listen while the collection plate move from one person to the next.

When my dad saw the ushers disperse the plates, he got a check from his wallet and pulled a pen from his shirt pocket to fill out the check. My wife and I heard something that sounded like a dog's whimper, and we turned to the right toward dad. He was looking puzzled as his hands were covered in blue ink from the leaky pen. As he looked at us in bewilderment, he held his hand out much like a little boy who had broken a favorite toy. I took the check and filled it out while dad was trying to figure out how to get all of the ink off of his hands.

Now my wife saw that he was having a problem and offered him some tissues. With satisfaction that he had been given the answer to his problem, he quickly proceeded to wipe off the ink. However, the ink didn't come off: it smeared into his skin, turning his fingers and hands a dark shade of blue. Each time he wiped, the ink was spread more. Yet, each time he saw the ink spread, he became more befuddled and agitated. I don't know if it was the operatic tenor trying to sing a gospel song with no accompaniment, the fact that my dad looked like a little boy who just had a bad accident, the intense displeasure on his face as he tried to wipe away the ink that just kept oozing, or a combination of all these events, but my wife started to laugh. Now, I don't mean one of those "bust a gut" belly laughs that one can do out in the open. I'm talking about one of those forbidden laughs that one can't be caught doing during weddings, funerals, or late-night Christmas services.

However, the more my wife tried to stop laughing, the more she couldn't stop as my dad kept wiping the ink off of his hands while, at the same time, emitting little grunts and groans of disgust. The only sound in the church was the singing of the tenor combined with an occasional congregant cough or creaky church pew. Soon, my wife was in full "silent laugh" mode as her face begin to turn red, tears welled up inside her eyes, and her hand was grasping her mouth ever so tightly.

I soon felt the pew start to quiver as my wife, while successful in holding back the noise of laughter, could not hold back the physical effects of it. She was slowly rocking back and forth on the pew while her body started to shake. She grasped my hand and squeezed it as she tried to compose herself.

Soon, the rest of the family felt the vibrations of the pew, bent forward a little, and looked to the right where we were sitting. Rather than be of assistance, I guess I didn't help matters much when I looked at both her and my dad in their play of predicaments. However, before my wife totally lost it and interrupted the quiet service with laughter, the tenor completed his song, the music died down, and my father quickly placed his hands in his pockets and looked up at the altar as if nothing had happened.

After the service when we all got in the car, my wife could finally tell everyone what had happened. As I drove away from the church and past the crowd of merry well-wishers and sparkling Christmas lights, I could still hear my dad grunting and groaning as he tried to wipe the ink from his hands while my wife was trying to suppress her impending burst of laughter as she tried to assist him. I thought to myself that this would be a church service I would not soon forget.

###

December 25

Christmas Sunday

In my life, there have only been nine times when Christmas actually fell on a Sunday. To me, this is a special time. It is a time when our reflections of what Christmas really means should be the most powerful and strong. I remember the thrill of getting up on Christmas morning to quickly look at what Santa brought us, eat a hot holiday breakfast, and then head off to celebrate the birth of Christ in God's house.

If you think about it, Easter, Mother's Day, and Father's Day always happen on a Sunday. However, Christmas always occurs on December 25th, so it travels through the days of the week as the years progress. Christmas falling on a Sunday is a rather unusual event. I would imagine that most people don't even know the last time Christmas was on a Sunday or when it will happen again.

I did a little research and found out from someone that this phenomenon is actually a cycle and it takes 28 years to complete. Within that cycle, however, Christmas will fall on a Sunday in 11 years, then six years, then five years, and then six years again.

Walking into the church on Christmas Sunday was a special treat. The day seemed a little brighter, people seemed happier, and the music sounded a little sweeter. The pastor was usually dressed in his white Christmas robe and stole, while the choir greeted everyone with a joyous Christmas song to welcome the day. If you were lucky enough to be at a church with bells, you could hear them pealing their bright, clear sounds through the frosty morning air.

People dressed in their red, green, and white wished each other a "Merry Christmas" as they sat in the pews, while children sat anxiously awaiting the services to end so they to get back home to enjoy their toys and candy. Usually this special Sunday brought a lot of guests as relatives of church members, who came from far-away places, would visit our church to ring in the special day and to worship the Christ Child.

As the sun shone through multi-colored stained glass windows, candles were burning brightly in the window sills and on the altar. Beside the altar was the Advent Wreath. Only four Sundays ago, we lit the first of four purple candles. Now, in addition to those, a large white candle in the center of the wreath (known as the Christmas Candle) had been lit. The rich green garland hung throughout the church was punctuated with bright red bows. The large tree adorned with all of its embroidered Christmons told of the birth and life of Jesus. The opening hymn during a Christmas Sunday service was usually "Hark, The Herald Angles Sing," or "Joy to the World." The large organ would play the introduction as the congregation stood in reverence and sang strongly and joyfully. The pastor would then open his bible and read the Christmas Story from either Matthew or Luke. After the choir sang their special song, the pastor would immediately go into his sermon.

I would look around and see people with warm smiles on their faces, sitting close to their loved ones. Fathers and mothers would usually have some silent Christmas toy on standby to pacify the animated minds and bodies of their young children. Occasionally, I could hear the distinctive sound of cellophane crinkling as Christmas candy was unwrapped to the delight of a young child or eager grandparent.

When the service was over, the organ belted out a familiar Christmas hymn as church members wished each other a blessed day. The candles were extinguished as the pastor shook everyone's hands as they filed out of the church. Soon everyone headed home for Christmas dinners, parties, and packages to give and unwrap.

As a boy, I always loved Christmas on Sunday. I never wanted it to end. As I grew older, I questioned why this day should be treated so special, though. I mean, after all, shouldn't we celebrate the birth of Christ more than one day a year? Shouldn't we live with the spirit of Christmas in our hearts the entire year?

Now, most don't dress up to go to church on Christmas. Many people don't even bother attending church at all when Christmas falls on a Sunday. In fact, many churches have now decided not to hold church services in order to give families time to be together. I don't understand this reasoning. Wouldn't a church be the best place to be with family during Christmas on Sunday? Using that same logic, why don't we shut down churches on Easter?

This year I'm not going let the hustle and bustle of gift buying, decorating, going to parties, and visiting with friends and relatives cause me to forget the real reason we celebrate Christmas. I look forward to dressing up with my family, going to church, celebrating the birth of Jesus, and spreading the joy of the Christ Child to others. After all, isn't Jesus the reason for the season?

###

December 26

The Christmas Dinner

Nowhere was a Christmas celebration more enthusiastically embraced than dinner at my grandmother's house in Florence, Alabama. As a young boy, I thought it was the most spectacular event our family had. Not only was it a time to celebrate the season, we were also able to reunite with relatives we hadn't seen since the year before or longer. Everyone looked forward to it, and year after year, we were never disappointed.

For me, the dinner usually started early in the morning with the smell of bread, pies, or cakes baking in the oven. I would stumble out of bed and walk into the kitchen to see my grandmother adorned with her favorite apron and whistling while she performed the multitude of tasks before her. After breakfast, I always wanted to help her. I was a small boy, however, and although she usually gave me some small task like putting silverware on the table, there was not much I could do but watch.

While she was cooking, I usually snuck into the dining room to check out where the feast would take place. There was a large oval oak table that took up most of the room. Around it where assorted chairs because there were not enough of the same style chairs to seat all of the guests. In the center of the table was a green bayberry pillar candle encircled with holy and red berries. Throughout the table were Christmas salt and pepper shakers, small little decorations, and grandmother's nicest china. Against the wall was a sideboard where many of the pies and cakes waited to be eaten.

During this time, every corner of grandmother's house smelled of bread, sage, onion, turkey, ham, vanilla, and cinnamon. One could almost satisfy the appetite by taking a deep breath. Just when I thought my hunger would overtake me, the relatives started to arrive. First was my Aunt Biddy and Uncle Charlie. She was a proper southern lady with an infectious laugh who was a school teacher and who also baked the best chocolate pound cake I have ever eaten. Uncle Charlie was a balding, boisterous, and gregarious man who had a warm smile and smart wit.

They had three children who were much older than I. Jeb was always the gentleman who was a talented singer and who was also very intelligent. He later became a doctor. His brother, Blair, had the smile and comedic nature of his father. He was accepted into the Air Force Academy, and every time I saw him, I always wondered what secret mission he was involved with that he couldn't divulge. Their sister, Nancy, was always very pretty and spent a good bit of time playing games with me in the parlor.

Next came my Aunt Mary Elizabeth and Uncle Bob. To me, she always looked like a movie star. She had a deep rich southern accent and was always perfectly dressed. Uncle Bob interested me greatly. He was a chemist who actually worked on the Manhattan Project. Although he never talked about his work in detail, my imagination wandered as to what important work he might be doing.

My grandmother had very pretty gray hair that was always fixed no matter how hard she worked. When I saw my grandmother, the first thing I noticed was her smile. It was so warm and expressive that it caused her eyes to sparkle and cheeks to blush. Along with my grandmother was her sister, Nina, who lived with grandmother in the house. Nina looked frail and small walking from room to room with her cane or walker, but what she lacked in physic, she made up for in personality. She could easily go toe-to-toe with my Uncle Charlie and leave him begging for mercy.

As the years progressed, my cousins brought their wives and families with them, and somehow, we always made room around that big table for everyone. While there was no specific seating arrangements, my grandmother usually sat at the end of the table, closest to the kitchen, and my dad sat at the other end. I usually liked to sit as close as I could to my grandmother.

Now, the feast was nothing of great extravagance. While delicious and massive, it usually consisted of the typical turkey, ham, rolls, corn, green bean casserole, butter peas, and various kinds of congealed salad. I guess about the only time the food became part of our Christmas dinner memories was when, one year, my aunt passed the green bean casserole over to my dad. The casserole was in one of those glass dishes that was inserted into a silver carry base with handles on each end. That year, my father took the casserole, and as he moved it over to his plate, one of the handles broke, and the entire casserole landed in his lap. After the initial shock, everyone laughed. I was delighted because I didn't really care for green bean casserole, and I quickly spooned more corn on my plate to take its place.

The most important part of those dinners were the various conversations that took place around that table. In the collective known simply as "the family," we could rival Hollywood executives in critiquing the latest movies. We could astonish the scientific community with our new postulates on natural phenomenon. We could defy world leaders with our innate knowledge of foreign affairs. We could amaze government officials by how we could more effectively run City Hall. In short, all of the world's problems could be, and quite often were, solved around that table. During that dinner, everyone had an equal voice, including myself as the youngest. In fact, it was expected that we all should join in the conversation.

Most importantly, however, Dad was the owner of "the list." When someone would irritate him on television or in government, he would always threaten to put his or her name on "the list." Now, mind you, as it turned out there was nothing very particular about his list – although as a young child, I saw it as a most powerfully poignant instrument, and I never had the nerve to ask what he ever intended to do with it. I later found out to my relief that "the list" never actually existed. However, if a radical politician upset my Aunt Nina, she would rap her cane a few times on the floor, shake her finger in the air, and exclaim "Hey Ben…put him on your list."

Now, we were a mixed family. Sometimes that fact caused a little consternation. During the 60's and 70's in Alabama, a mixed family meant that half of us cheered on Bear Bryant and the Alabama Crimson Tide while the other half cheered on Shug Jordan and the War Eagles of Auburn University. Sometimes the conversation could take a bold and unexpected turn as my Uncle Charlie would cock his hawkish eye toward my father and prognosticate over his peas how Auburn could win the national championship. My dad would just look at him, shake his head, and then slather his roll with another pat of butter. We were never too hard core over this subject, though, and my dad and Uncle Charlie would always strongly pull for whichever Alabama team really had a chance at the national title.

After dinner, the desserts went around, and because it was Christmas, I was allowed to have more than one piece of these delectable dishes. While there were the usual holiday cakes and pies, inevitably one of the women in our family would bring a new dessert whose recipe she had found in a women's magazine. Everyone would comment on its uniqueness of taste and/or texture, and some of the women would ask for the recipe. Sometimes, these new desserts would make it into the annual fare. Other times they would be dismissed to only a faint memory on our taste buds.

At the end of dinner, the grown-ups would help take everything to the kitchen while my cousin Nancy and I went to the parlor to watch television or play games. After all of the food was put up and the dishes put away, we all loaded into one of several vehicles to drive a few miles over to my Aunt Biddy and Uncle Charlie's house to gather by the tree in her living room to exchange gifts. If the dinner conversation was especially lively that year, it would usually follow us into my aunt's living room.

Every time I pass by the house that used to be my grandmother's, I always pause briefly and look toward the window of that dining room. If I close my eyes, I can almost hear my dad and Uncle Charlie talking about politics and football while my aunts laugh amid the clanking and clinking of dinnerware. While I miss those old times, I'm thankful for all the fond memories.

###

December 27

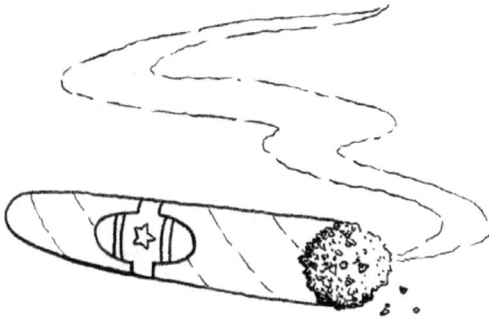

Christmas Ghost

No collection of Christmas stories would be complete without a ghost story. Now, the most famous of all holiday ghost stories is *A Christmas Carol* by Charles Dickens. However, a long time ago, ghost stories where a staple of the festive celebration of Christmas.

In England during Victorian times, the practice of gathering around the hearth-fire on Christmas Eve to tell ghost stories was as much a part of the holidays as Santa Claus, mistletoe, or singing Christmas carols is for us today.

"Whenever five or six English-speaking people meet round a fire on Christmas Eve, they start telling each other ghost stories," wrote British humorist, Jerome K. Jerome as part of his introduction to an anthology of Christmas ghost stories titled *Told After Supper*, in 1891. "Nothing satisfies us on Christmas Eve but to hear each other tell authentic anecdotes about specters."

Before I relate my little ghost story – if a ghost is what I actually saw – a little background information is needed. My family's history goes way back in Florence, Alabama. My great-great grandfather, Zebulon P. Morrison, was the mayor of the town back in 1855. His wife, Biddy, was the daughter of an Irish immigrant who came to the area as an engineer of the first lock on that part of the Tennessee River. Mr. Morrison built the first building on the campus of the current University of North Alabama and made it look like a castle in homage to his wife who missed them when she left Ireland.

Mr. and Mrs. Morrison had eleven children. One, Winona (known endearingly as Winny), met James Blair. They later married and built a white Victorian house on the corner of East Mobile Street and Walnut Street in the downtown area next to Winny's father. This is the house where my grandmother, Adele, was born and lived and where we would visit for many Christmases.

When my grandmother was young, she went off to school in Nashville to become a teacher. While there, she met my grandfather, Benjamin, and in 1914 they were married on Christmas Eve in the room that served as a library in the house where my grandmother was born and lived. The library adjoined a large dining room and was separated by a large pocket door. My grandfather moved down to Florence, and he and my grandmother lived in the house with her parents. My grandparents had three children, my father and two aunts. My grandfather passed away long before I was born.

Dad used to tell me that, as a boy, he had a collection of metal toy soldiers that he used to play with in the parlor as his father watched in excitement. He would often comment to dad about the large army he had amassed. In truth, whenever dad would have some extra money from his paper route, he would run down to Woolworth's Department store to buy one or two more soldiers.

Another story my dad told me concerned a ritual that my grandfather practiced. Every Saturday, without fail, my grandfather would walk a few blocks over to Anderson's News Stand where he would buy a magazine and a cigar for Sunday after church. According to my dad, his father could always been seen out on the porch of his house every Sunday puffing his cigar and reading his magazine as the sun disappeared slowly in the western sky.

Now, here is my little ghost story…

The year was 1967, and I was eight years old. My family left Tuscaloosa early in the afternoon on Christmas Day for the two-and-a-half hour drive up to Florence. When we got there, we turned the corner from Tennessee Street to Walnut, and a couple of blocks down, I could see my grandmother standing by the large bay window in the parlor awaiting our arrival.

When I got out of the car, grandmother was at the back door. I greeted her with a warm, hearty hug. She always smelled of baked goods and fresh soap, and being around her pleased me greatly. As we all gathered in the kitchen, grandmother told us that more family members than usual were coming and we would have to work out different sleeping arrangements. While I usually slept in the upstairs corner room, I would now be sleeping with my grandmother. Because she had been renting part of the upstairs to a college student for many years, she moved her bedroom to the first floor where the library used to be.

As we did for many Christmases, we all ate dinner at grandmother's house on Christmas evening and then loaded up the cars and drove down to my aunt's house to "have the tree." This was when we all exchanged gifts and each one of us had to open only one gift at a time. By the time the final gift was unwrapped and we had our final treat of my grandmother's boiled custard and my aunt's chocolate pound cake, the evening was late. We headed back to grandmother's house for bed and rest.

While grandmother was still in the kitchen doing the dishes and whistling her happy little tune, I changed into my pajamas, turned out the lights, and tucked myself in for a long night's rest. On the mantel in grandmother's room was an old clock in which the rhythmic tick-tock, tick-tock sounded louder than usual. On that particular Christmas, it was not very cold outside. However, the wind blew through the trees and rattled the house. The street light partly shown through grandmother's window, and along with observing the mantel clock, I could see all of the old pictures of relatives long since passed away that were hanging on the wall.

Whether it was the blowing of the wind or the flickering of the street light through the trees, the eyes from all of my relatives in those pictures seemed to be looking directly at me. Toward the left of the clock was the picture of my grandfather. He was wearing a vested suit and had a stern, stately look on his face. That night, all of those pictures somehow looked eerie and menacing in the darkness of grandmother's room. I remember that I turned over on my side and looked at the giant wardrobe against the wall until I fell asleep.

When I awoke, the mantle clock chimed six times. I looked out the window. It was surprising to me that I was only 6 a.m. and yet it was so bright outside. While I thought about getting out of bed, I was warm and comfortable and wanted to go back to sleep. However, looking around the room, things had changed. The room seemed to go back to the library rather than my grandmother's bedroom. There were books and bookcases around the room. I saw the *Harvard Classics* prominently displayed on a built-in shelf inside the wall, and there was a nice mission-style desk where papers and books were strewn.

I then saw a man walk into the room. He was medium height, dressed in a vested suit, and held a cigar in his mouth. At this point, I was more startled than scared, and I looked to see where he would go or what he might do. He walked directly to the far window and looked out onto East Mobile Street.

"It's almost sundown, and Sonny's got his army out on the porch playing," he said as he pulled his pants up a little while taking a draw from his cigar. "I believe I'll go out there with him and read my magazine." As he walked out of the room, I could hear him say, "That boy has enough of those soldiers to make a full-fledged army." At that point, the only scent lingering in the room was the smell of his cigar.

I turned over in the bed and remembered that my dad used to be called Sonny when he was small. I also remembered that the man said it was six in the evening rather than six in the morning. For a moment, I was shocked that I had slept that long. However, my tiredness overcame me, and I fell fast to sleep. When I woke up again, it was almost eight in the morning. I heard grandmother in the kitchen cooking breakfast. I looked around the room and saw that it had reverted back to a bedroom and everything was in its place as it was before I went to bed.

As I crawled out of bed, I believed that I must have had some weird dream. I never really saw the face of the man who came into the room. I could only smell the smoke from his cigar. I looked up at all of the pictures of my relatives, and they didn't look as eerie in the morning light. At that point, I resolved that it was a dream, and I proceeded to forget about it and go on my merry way. After all, I had toys and games that I had received the night before that needed to be played with. I never told anyone about that dream.

The rest of the day was uneventful. I played with my toys, watched a little football with the family, and ate a lot of Christmas leftovers. About six in the evening when I was in the parlor watching television, my dad walked in with two old, large boxes. He offered them to me and told me that he had just been in the attic and he decided that I was old enough to take care of and be responsible for the contents inside.

Imagine my surprise when I opened the boxes and saw dozens and dozens of metal WWI-Era toy soldiers. It was a sight to behold! The rest of that evening, he sat on the floor with me, and we pulled out each one of the soldiers as he told me stories about them. It was neat to see the excitement on his face as we played with the soldiers together, and it was clear to see that he did have enough soldiers to have an entire army. As a boy of eight, I thought it was strange that I had a dream about a man walking in the library of the house at six in the evening talking about dad's soldiers and at six the next evening, my dad had pulled the toy soldiers down from grandmother's attic to give to me. In the dream, I never saw the man nor the soldiers that he talked about. While I also didn't see the boy he was talking about, I just assumed it was my dad.

Was it just my imagination? Did I overhear dad talk about the toy soldiers without realizing it, and I involuntarily created a whimsical dream? Did all of the stories I'd hear about my dad and grandfather culminate into some type of subconscious state that was triggered when I saw the picture of my grandfather on the wall? Or, was I really visited by my grandfather? I don't know.

I went to bed that night tired from all of the day's excitement. Grandmother's bedroom was dark, and the streetlight and trees threw dappled shadows into the room. I heard the rhythmic tick-tock, tick-tock of the mantel clock, and I saw the faces of my relatives as their pictures hung above the mantle above me. Again, the picture of my grandfather in his vested suit looked down at me. However, tonight, he didn't appear as stern as the night before, and for a brief moment, I thought I caught a whiff of cigar smoke as I drifted off to sleep.

###

December 28

Letter from Santa

*M*y *children made it a habit of leaving a letter for Santa right beside his milk and cookies each Christmas Eve night. I was surprised to see that they were not asking for toys or other goodies. Rather, they simply had some questions about the North Pole, the elves, Mrs. Claus, and especially Santa himself. They wanted to know how he was doing, how old he was, and how he could carry all those toys by himself. My children were surprised that Santa took the time to write back. Later, as the years progressed, they looked forward to their mutual communications. Below is one such letter from Santa that he wrote to them when Jay and Jessica crossed over from being children to teenagers…*

Jay and Jessica:
Ho! Ho! Ho!

Merry Christmas and I hope you enjoy what I brought you from the North Pole. Thanks for the milk, cookies and especially, your letter. I appreciate you comparing me to Jesus because I try to live my life doing what Jesus wants me to do. All of us should do that every day of our lives. Unfortunately, many children only see me and the gifts I bring. They fail to see that this day is Jesus' birthday and that He is the most special gift to all of us from God.

Jay and Jessica, it clearly seems that you two are beginning to understand what Christmas is all about. As you said in your letter, Christmas is more about giving than receiving. Although I will not be able to get you everything you wanted, I hope that you really like what I brought you because you have been good children at school and home. I also appreciate the way that you share your gifts and toys with each other as well as get along with each other.

Now, this year marks a very special and wonderful time in your lives. Next year, you will be 13 and will no longer be considered children anymore. There are many wonderful surprises ahead of you as you grow older, and I will always be watching you every year.

In growing older, however, you will also notice some changes. Some of these changes are physical, and some happen because of where you are in life. Unfortunately, one of those changes is that I will no longer visit your house each year as I have done in the past.

You see, Santa Clause visits the homes of good little children to deliver gifts and other goodies. I can only do this for children. Since both of you have grown up, you are no longer children anymore. I have to move on to all the new children who were born this year. This doesn't mean that I love you any less. Quite the contrary, I love you even more because you have learned the lesson of giving gifts yourself, and you will find many wonderful moments as you exchange gifts with your friends and family.

Have you ever noticed how, as you get older, the gifts you receive are smaller in size. When you are very young, the presents you get are big and magnificent. As you get older, the types of gifts you receive are very different from the ones you received when you were a child, but they will become more important to you. Soon the desire to get a gift weakens as your desire to give a gift grows. While you are still too young to fully realize this blessing, as you grow older, you will experience the unique and fulfilling joy and excitement that only comes from giving.

Jay and Jessica, from the time you were born till now, I've known that you were very special people who are filled with God's light. As you get older, I hope that you will use this light to bring light to others through the giving of yourselves. That is the true spirit of Christmas. I ask you to always remember to keep this spirit in your heart now and forever more.

While I may not visit your house each year anymore, I'm still around looking after all of my children…both young and old. As you get older and find that special person you want to love, care for, and plan your own family with, who knows,

I may come to your house again one day with a very, very special gift for the two of you. Until then, Jay and Jessica, have a very merry Christmas and always keep the true spirit of Christmas in your heart.

Santa

###

December 29

The Empty House

After my father passed away, my mom tried staying in her home in Northport, Alabama, for over four years before she decided to sell the house and move down to Florida with my sister. Everything happened very quickly regarding planning the move, selling her possessions, and getting the house on the market. My job kept me very busy during those couple of months, and I was unable to assist her. When I finally did get to see the house, my mom had already left for Florida, and the place was completely empty. Walking around the bare rooms, I saw the house that had been such a big part of my life for the past 50 years in a completely different light. It was strange.

I went into the den and looked around where our furniture used to be. I walked up to the mantel above the fireplace, and my eyes focused on something very small but very poignant. Underneath the mantle were little holes where the hooks were inserted to hang our Christmas stockings. For a moment, I could almost see them hanging, filled to the brim, next to the brightly colored decorations that mom usually had on top of the mantle. As I turned around, I suddenly felt that I was a small boy again during Christmas Eve standing in my flannel pajamas as dad pointed the movie camera toward me holding my stocking while mom held the bright lights above him.

I then walked into the dining room half expecting to see our table fully adorned in all its Christmas best with dad leaning over the turkey to make sure enough had been carved on the plate for all to enjoy. As I closed my eyes, I could faintly smell mom's homemade cornbread dressing with the distinct aromas of sage and onions permeating the room. Opening my eyes, however, all was gone like the flames from the candles we snuffed out after our holiday dinner. The room was dark and empty.

I turned to go into the living room and looked over to the far corner where our Christmas tree always stood. I could almost see the colored lights of the tree dancing magically on the walls and ceiling of the room. For a brief moment, I remembered the year that my parents bought a real tree and one of our cats decided to climb it. I remembered running into the living room to find the tree lying across the floor. After that accident, we never could get that tree to stand straight for the rest of the holiday.

I turned to the left to see where dad's pedestal desk sat next to the picture window. This is where mom set up our Christmas village. I remembered the balsam wood cabin and the incense smoke that came out of its chimney and wondered where that little cabin was now. I remembered that, no matter how hard we tried, we couldn't get our cat to stay off the village. Every night during the holidays when I would go into the living room to sit by the tree, I would see her curled up on top of the village next to the cabin and the mirror pond where our skaters frolicked. Clearly the cat didn't fit the scale of our village and oftentimes looked like a monster invading the tiny hamlet.

I then looked at the bare, carpeted floor where my Christmas presents usually were placed. I could almost see my Major Matt Mason space station, Varoom Bicycle, and new BB gun laying there. I remember that I usually woke up very early to find what Santa had brought me and I was careful not to wake up my parents. I noticed that, even in the empty house, I still walked softly so as to not awake the people no longer there.

I walked down to the end of the hall to my first bedroom. As I looked at the emptiness of it, I remembered one particular Christmas Eve night when I went to bed full of anticipation of what Santa would bring me the next day. I remembered that it was very cold outside and my soft pajamas were warm as I slid beneath the sheets. Dad came in my room as he always did and read a story to me before turning out the light. I remembered that night well because the moon was almost full and its light was shining through my window.

I lay in my bed wide awake and wondering if I would be able to actually see Santa this year. One of my windows was next to my bed, and because my parents were in the bedroom next to me, I was very quiet as I moved over to open the curtain and look outside. My young eyes wandered over the sky to find any sign. Maybe a red nose glaring. But the bed was too warm and comfortable, and soon I fell fast asleep. Now, the curtains are gone in the empty room, and the window doesn't seem as large as it once did.

I walked the vacant hall back to the stairs that took me down to the basement. During one special Christmas, I spent a lot of time decorating the large downstairs room. I put up my little five foot tree and wrapped the entire room in lighted garland. After dinner at a nice restaurant, I took my soon-to-be wife downstairs where the warmth of a fire and the lights of the Christmas decorations made the entire room cozy, and festive. That was the night that I proposed to her and she accepted. Now, looking around the empty basement, I caught a glimpse of a solitary wire hanger dangling from the ceiling that I used to hang up that garland almost 35 years ago.

I walked back up the stairs and went back into the living room. When I got married, we always continued the Luna tradition of "having the tree" in that living room. I could faintly see bows, wrapping paper, and boxes all over the floor as we all celebrated the season together. I remember one Christmas when my dad opened a gift addressed to him. He pulled out a pair of powder-blue, loose-fitting pants. While he looked a little surprised and puzzled, he thanked the giver and remarked on their "pretty blue color." We then soon realized that the pants were meant for my mom. While dad leaned back in his chair with the signs of relief in his eyes, we all laughed out loud and gave him another gift to open.

All of these Christmas memories and more flooded my mind and lifted my spirits one minute, only to be interrupted by the pangs of sadness the very next. This will soon no longer be my house. I will never share another Christmas joy here again. Everything was now gone in my house except my memories of a half century of Christmases.

As I walked out the door and closed it for the very last time, I was saddened by the fact that so much of my life seemed like it had been packed up and moved out of that house never to be seen again. While I know that this sort of thing happens to others as parents move out of their houses, it is actually terrible when it happens to you.

As I got in my car I was comforted by all of my fond memories and the fact that a house is only a home when loved ones are there. Nobody lives at my parents' house now, and it is cold, empty, and desolate. I drove off to go to my own home in Florence, Alabama, where my family and I would soon spend Christmas together.

###

December 30

The Christmas Star

There is something inspiring about going for a walk on a clear, brisk evening during Christmastime. Gazing at the colored lights adorning the doors, windows, and trees around nearby houses, or catching a whiff of wood smoke from a distant chimney, I quickly fall into a joyous seasonal mood and often start to wonder.

On one of those nights, it was especially clear. The stars hung bright in the cold, dark sky as if I could almost reach out and touch them, and the icy air frosted my breath and numbed my ears as I continued to look up at the sky.

I couldn't help but think of that very first Christmas light: the Star of Bethlehem. The more I looked at the stars, the more my logical mind tried to envision that wonderful phenomenon that guided the Wise Men to the Baby Jesus. What was this star? How did it shine so bright for such a short time and then extinguish itself as if it had never existed?

Some have explained the star as a comet. Others have said that it was a rare instance where the planet Jupiter was aligned just right with the earth so as to create a bright orb of light. Some have even said that the star never actually existed. Rather, it was either a fallacy or metaphor.

Now, if you believe in God, and I hope you do, you will believe that He is capable of creating a comet, arranging the planets in a special way, or simply putting anything up there in the sky that He wanted. In fact, for just that short period of time, He could have created a new bright star that would shortly diminish after it served its purpose. My theory, however, is a little different, but quite fascinating in its meaning.

It seems that some scientists have discovered the remains of a supernova that would have been seen on Earth about the time of Christ's birth. A supernova occurs when a star blows up and its light is so bright it can shine across galaxies. They are common, although, we don't see many of them. So, why is this phenomenon so special to this story? Why would this particular supernova be so prophetic?

To understand all of this, one must first understand the distance of stars in our universe and the concept of the light year. Light travels very fast at 156,000 miles per second, and a light year is how many miles light will travel in a year's time. To do the calculations, it is estimated that in one light year, light will travel almost five trillion miles. Therefore, the light from an explosion five trillion miles away from Earth will take about a year before the human eye can actually see it. This is much like the gap of time that exists when you see a boy hit a ball far away, only to hear the crack of his bat seconds later.

Now, it is obvious that the Sun is the closest star to Earth. However, the next closest star to the Sun is *Alpha Centauri,* which is approximately 4.24 light years or almost 60 trillion miles away.

So, why is all of this important to the birth of Christ? If the scientists are correct and the star over Bethlehem was actually a supernova, the closest one of these to Earth was over 250,000 light years away. In other words, the supernova in question occurred at least a quarter of a million years before the birth of Christ. That means after traveling space for millennia, the light from that exploding star made it to Earth exactly on that special night for man to see and use as a guide.

To me, this phenomenon is not coincidental and demonstrates the awesome power of God. Within the Old Testament, the prophets foretold the coming of Christ. They somehow knew that this event would eventually unfold, though they did not know when. God knew, however. In fact, if my theory is correct, God created the supernova that appeared over the baby Jesus hundreds of thousands of years before man ever walked the earth. Think of how amazing and prophetic that is.

Pondering this theory, I felt even smaller as I stood out underneath all those stars. What has God already done for us? What will God do for us in the future? It boggles the mind. However, as I made my way through the cold, lonely darkness of the night, a warm smile came over me because I knew that God is forever with me, and while I can enjoy a guess or two as to what He may be up to, his secrets will never be fully revealed.

###

December 31

The Christmas Tree

It's Christmas time, and after dinner, I take my chair by the
fire.
I admire our pretty Christmas tree in all its great attire.
The tree's warm glow and cheerfulness add contrast to a
night,
When the north wind blows, the snow falls down on a blanket, cold and white.
The garland glitters, the ornaments sparkle against the
multi-colored light,
That old tree tells of holidays past; I reminisce in pure delight.

Up and down my eyes wander 'round every inch of that ole
tree;
Then suddenly I realize something that, till now, I'd only yet
to see.
The tree is like a pyramid where larger limbs lie below,
It tapers up where the smaller limbs cradle a star of golden
glow.
I now realize that my old tree represents this life of mine,
Of past and future, my story told from this old Christmas
pine.
When I was a boy, I wanted toys and stuff too long to list,
Those larger branches were there to hold all my childhood
Christmas gifts.
As I got older, my gifts got smaller but still, most were all
about me,
Until I learned that giving is better; it was the middle of my
tree.
Then one Christmas, I offered her a golden ring as my sym-
bol of unfailing love.
My limbs now were shorter, but they held special gifts, of a
love that comes from above.
Through my children, wife, and others, I now want only to
give,
My branches they grow smaller, but richer, the longer I live.
As my years wind down, the star shines brighter and now I
truly see:
Jesus' precious gift of life everlasting is shown from my ole
Christmas tree.

###

www.ingramcontent.com/pod-product-compliance
Lightning Source LLC
Chambersburg PA
CBHW051840090426
42736CB00011B/1890